FOR KEEPS

FOR KEEPS

A WINDOW INTO THE FASCINATING WORLD OF ZOOKEEPING

Noel Harcourt

NEW HOLLAND

First published in 2025 by New Holland Publishers

newhollandpublishers.com

A record of this book is held at the National Library of Australia.

ISBN 9781760797911

Managing Director: Fiona Schultz
General Manager/Publisher: Olga Dementiev
Designer: Andrew Davies
Production Director: Arlene Gippert

Keep up with New Holland Publishers:

NewHollandPublishers
@newhollandpublishers

To my daughter and son,

Chloe and Simon,

who like me, have turned

their passions into professions,

and to my father Con,

who inspired me with his love of books,

and his phrase that

"If something is worth doing,

it is worth doing well."

CONTENTS

PROLOGUE

"You should write a book" became the standard response I would get during an evening out with friends, when the conversation would no doubt end up being about Melbourne Zoo. People always wanted to know what was happening and hear stories, some repeated many times, of births, escapes or other relevant interesting issues that happened in a zookeeper's daily working life. So on hearing "you should write a book" so many times over the years, I decided to heed the advice, and write it all down. At first I thought that it would be something to write down as a memoir to pass onto family members, but as it grew I began to look at it as something more, something for everyone to read. So I began writing it all down many years ago when I was still employed at the zoo, picking it up from time to time, making corrections and adding to it. Coming across the file that I kept it in from time to time after leaving the zoo, I wondered at one time if it was worth continuing with. Then at the beginning of 2023 I decided once and for all to make a serious effort in putting it all together and finally completing it. So here it is, without any exaggerations or embellishments, as it all happened. I hope you enjoy reading it all as much as I did recalling and writing it down over many years, and it gives me great solace in knowing that it is now down in writing, "FOR KEEPS".

CHAPTER 1

When You Least Expect It, Expect It!

When you least expect it, expect it, was a common phrase I would always use to remind myself, and others I was working with or training on any Animal Department within the zoo, that you only have a split second due to a lack of concentration or an interruption to let an animal out, or walk out into an enclosure with one. Training on dangerous Animal Rounds was both extensive and intensive, and it was the Big Cat round that a keeper would be trained on last, on the Carnivore Department, after proving their ability to work with other carnivores on the other rounds. Each keeper had a radio so they could be contacted at any time, if a keeper was late for a break or lunch they would be contacted on the radio to ensure that they were ok. Each radio had a 'Man Down' alarm feature, that would activate if left in a horizontal position for any length of time. It was not the intention of the Man Down alarm that would or could save you, but it would allow colleagues to know where to find you dead or injured. There always had been that voice that you would pay attention to when it came down to safety measures, checking the locks and sometimes double checking. Making sure that you are always well aware of where that big cat is, and that it is safely secured and does not have access to the area that you are entering. It all in the end comes down to human error, that has cost the lives of keepers in other zoos, some that I had previously worked with. It was also very important to be aware that repetitive tasks didn't become that, and that each task was deliberate.

So it happened that one day I sat in the big cat keeper off-limit area with my head in my hands, trembling uncontrollably, with those very thoughts racing through my mind. For it could have been a very different outcome, if I had chosen to ignore that inner voice. I was under pressure that day, it had been a very busy morning and the last exhibit for me to service housed a female snow leopard called Meo. Snow leopards are fast, agile, and incredibly strong. They frequent high mountainous terrains at elevations of some 4000 meters. They have short forelimbs and long hind legs, and are capable of leaping up to 9 meters, six times their own body length. I had gone through the usual routine of checking that Meo was within her night den, and that the access shute door to her off-limit area was closed. While still allowing too much to be on my mind, I entered the enclosure to service it, knowing that her faeces would be in the usual spot at the far end where she always defecated. Halfway in I looked across to see that the shute door to the off-limit yard was open. That's when that voice within told me to exit and check, when I could have so easily proceeded. I then left the area and upon securing the display I looked into Meo's night den via the mesh viewing window, only to see her at the open off-limit access shute door, watching me, where she had full access to the display and me. If it wasn't for the fact that she was a very nervous cat, or if it had been any of the other snow leopards, it could have been a fatal outcome, with this book never being written.

Several days later after some 33 years of service at Melbourne Zoo under my belt I decided to take nine months accumulated long service leave and give myself time to look back upon my career at the zoo and make a decision as to my future within it. Not that I felt that I could no longer work within the zoo, but at almost 65 years old I felt that the maybe it was time to make some changes to my life. The zoo at the time had changed considerably, and the carnivore collection was not as expansive as it had been. This in itself wasn't a negative issue, but I felt that maybe the time had come where I had nothing more to offer the zoo and it had nothing more to offer me. One after all would have to be naive to think that things won't change and move in different directions after 33-odd years in the workplace. So after taking long service leave I came to the conclusion that it was time to look at what was on the other side of the zoo wall. My career at Melbourne Zoo was an amazing experience and I've had the opportunity to work with some incredible animal species and equally incredible people – a time when we all worked together as a family and always looked out for one another in a career that many would envy.

CHAPTER 2

Where It All Began

I was born in 1952, the same year the Briggs family set up the Fun Fair at Melbourne Zoo. Also the Australian Big Hunters Club visited the zoo at that time, reasoning that they could assist in procuring animals for the zoo.

It all began for me as a young kid living in a quiet suburban street in Reservoir, where I built (with the help of my Dad's building skills) the backyard 'Menagerie'. If it swam, hissed, crawled, flew or climbed I kept it. From fish, birds, frogs, tortoises, lizards, snakes, invertebrates and even ferrets, one that managed to get hold of my finger through the wire of its cage one day which resulted in a very painful tug of war.

I prided myself on escorting visitors and relatives through my impressive growing collection, that even Noah would have been impressed with. As my collection of animals increased, we would often receive phone calls to inform me or my parents of an escapee in their driveway or back yard, which I would quickly race up the street to retrieve. I would often be found exploring areas in nearby creeks and catching caterpillars from the hedges that lined the street on the way home from school to add to my expanding collection. School show and tell sessions for me was to take along one of my lizards, which would always fetch screams from the female students, but impressed my teachers, one who came for a visit at our holiday house and went exploring with me to look at the local wildlife. I even converted my sister's disused play shed with the help from my Dad of course, into a bird aviary where I kept a few galahs. On one occasion I kept a young tiger snake in my bedroom with a tight-fitting lid on its enclosure, only for it to mysteriously disappear upon its discovery by my mother. I would have fish tanks with carp, found from the nearby Edwards Lake which I would visit often, with net in hand in the hope of catching that elusive fish. I would often visit the local aquarium and wonder at the numerous fish species within it. My bedroom wall was covered in animal posters and my bookcase strained under the weight of numerous natural history books. I would spend many a wet weekend sitting in my room reading about the natural world of wildlife. I would often be reminded at school that to find a career in the animal field would require much commitment, even to the extent of being informed by one of the teachers that the possibility of that happening to me was either very slim or not going to happen at all. But I never allowed this to deter me, in fact it just made me more determined. I lived completely enthralled by the animal world and would spend endless hours reading or visiting the local library to quench my insatiable thirst. I would spend hour after hour at our holiday property at Ballarat scooping out nets full of tadpoles or fishing for yabbies at the nearby dam, arriving back to the house with my newly acquired specimens.

CHAPTER 3

A Slice of Melbourne Zoo History

The Zoological society of Victoria began in 1857. Bourke and Wills set off from the site on their epic and tragic journey in 1862. Parkville at the time was little more than undeveloped grazing land. It was moved to the present site after the original site proved unsuitable. Baron Ferdinand Von Mueller orchestrated the layout of the Zoo and was the Victorian Government Botanist from 1857 to 1873. While this was all happening the Acclimatisation Society of Victoria was formed by Edward Wilson who had been editor of the Argus newspaper. The Acclimatisation Society and the Zoological Society amalgamated in 1861. By 1863 a fence had been constructed around the perimeter and animals had somewhat of a more permanent home. In 1866 a collection of lions and bears arrived, and from 1877 to 1900 the first elephant was offered to the Zoological Society but was deemed too expensive. At one stage two dogs got into the gardens and destroyed twelve wallabies, four kangaroos and some sheep, fire also destroyed the reptile house and all its occupants. A trip was planned to Sumatra and Indonesia to obtain large animals as added attractions to the zoo. The first concert was held in the gardens. As part of the centenary celebrations an Aboriginal encampment was set up as an exhibit. The zoo started to celebrate animals' birthdays and births as an added attraction for visitors. Taxidermy displays became a popular attraction. At the turn of the century a polar bear was acquired and lived for some 43 years within the zoo. Bisons arrived. The zoo strengthened its relations with circuses, in order to gain access to more animals. Many of the old wooden structures were replaced with concrete ones. In 1909 the zoo successfully bred brush turkeys, the first zoo to do so in the world. In 1912 attendances reached 390,000 visitors, the following year the first giraffe was acquired. In 1914 a leopard escaped and was found and shot in Brunswick, three Tasmanian Tigers were purchased. A terrier dog once entered the premises and began to attack the resident rat population, it was taken in by the zoo as the permanent rat exterminator. A polar bear escaped in 1925 and attacked a keeper who survived the ordeal, resulting in the walls of the bears enclosure being made higher. New buildings for the resident lions, tigers and leopards were built. During the great depression the zoo survived by caring for circus animals to generate funds. The Acclimatisation Society was taken over by the Zoological Board of Victoria. Attitudes began to change towards a better understanding of animals' habits due to Charles Darwin's book *On the Origin of Species*. Improvements were made to the feed stores, animal hospital and barns. The brick wall surrounding the zoo was constructed. The introduction of television created more attention and exposure for the zoo. The zoos new kiosk opened, and the moated monkey island was converted into a seal enclosure. An Orangutan, some Tasmanian devils and a monkey escaped the confines of their enclosures. So much had happened at the zoo up until the year I was born in 1952, and much more has evolved at the zoo since then.

My first visit to Melbourne Zoo was in 1960 at the ripe old age of 8, with my sister and father. We went on the carousel, which is still in existence and has had major renovation work done to it. There were also stagecoaches and other items you could climb over around the grounds. With fairy floss on sticks I roamed around the zoo totally enthralled by it all. The huge sulphur-crested cocky cage full of unwanted donated pets, the White Rabbit Castle and Bush Hut enclosures that not only contained rabbits of various colours and sizes but also the odd Guinea pig. The zoo also had a Persian domestic cat at one time; however it didn't take to a captive life at the zoo and died not long after it was acquired. Queenie the elephant would take kids for rides. A tractor would take visitors on zoo tours, disguised as a train that had an automated commentary, so the driver had to take the same route through the zoo over and over again. The train was sponsored by Peters Ice Cream, with large ice cream ads plastered all over its sides.

The zoo visit took place after we had visited my Mum in hospital and it was a worrying time for Mum and Dad, and the zoo trip enabled us to get our minds off things for a while. Mum was discharged several weeks later with a clean bill of health much to our relief.

It was years later when I was in high school that an opportunity arose for me to work at the zoo during the Christmas school holidays. The zoo at this time had just had the lion park built, this was in the day considered a state-of-the-art enclosure where the public could view lions on one side and African wild dogs on the other from a bridge that spanned the exhibit. At that time the tall wire fence in front of the elephant enclosure was replaced with a moat, giving visitors an uninterrupted view of the resident elephants. There were also large concrete big cat enclosures with steel barred fronts that contained an assortment of big cats from lions to leopards. The concrete back walls were roughly painted with a diorama that depicted a jungle or something similar, which didn't represent the animal's true environment at all, and the only shelter provided was a concrete cave where the occupant could get out of the weather but still be in full view. On one occasion while sweeping near the area, I witnessed a leopard which had managed to somehow get its claws into the leg of a wild dog in the adjoining cage. I believe that the wild dog in question had to be euthanised due to its massive leg injury. These out-of-date cages were later demolished. In 1972 the new big cat complex opened which concentrated on not only larger areas for the occupants, but more natural ones. Numerous foxes were housed in rather small wire cages with concrete caves in the middle. I can recall how they spent most of the time pacing back and forward, in the relatively small spaces. The Great Flight Aviary housed wedge-tailed eagles at the tallest end and a selection of sea birds at the other. There was also the large white concrete and steel fronted primate cage near the Reptile House that housed Baboons and gibbons. Some of the young monkeys could hang from the front bars and put out their hands in the hope that someone would offer them a treat. The Main Entrance also housed macaws and other bird species, incorporated into the area. There were several enclosures on the main drive that were built in 1923, still standing today. Some other buildings in the off-limit areas were used for Staff mess and change rooms, they still exist today and have been converted to state of the art veterinary facilities. In the early days Chimpanzees were housed in wire cages connected to the rear of the building, where visiting vets were warned not to park their vehicles too close to these cages at the risk of having them covered in chimp faeces, an activity that was often played out by the chimps.

My general zoo duties involved sweeping, raking and picking up rubbish discarded by irresponsible visitors, and other mundane tasks. Although there were numerous times I was caught out gazing at a group of primates or looking at the lions while leaning on my broom, sometimes pretending to be a keeper waiting for a member of the public to ask me a question which I was always eager to answer. At one time I jumped over the outer lower safety fence of the lion park to the main exhibit fence, to get as close to the lions as I could. They would no doubt react to me being there, but I always kept a safe distance away from them, hoping that someone would see me and believe that I was a keeper rather than a cleaner. One my favourite pastimes was to sit on the fence of the off-limit Pony Yard at lunch breaks and watch, and at times attempt to ride one of the ponies which were housed at the back of the elephant house. These were taken down on weekends to the Fun Fair for children to have pony rides, and for Christmas parties for zoo staff and their families. One occasion that I will always remember in those early days of my connection with the zoo was when I was given the task of cleaning the koala public viewing area, a semicircular asphalt pathway that visitors would walk through to get an uninterrupted view of the koalas. As I had only just started I wanted to impress the supervisor, who was rather a harsh and brisk individual, possibly due to the fact that he had been given the task of looking after and supervising us. I took my time in sweeping up every piece of rubbish, dirt and dust in that area and looked at the completed job with utmost pride, only to have Mr Harsh Supervisor walk up behind me asking me why I had taken so long to complete the job, and to move on to other dirty areas that required my immediate attention.

The work was mundane, repetitious, dusty, dirty and at times wet depending on the weather, and I would always look out for other tasks to do even though they were not on my to do list. At one time I overheard a group of gardeners discussing a planned trip to a local resident's garden to remove Giant Bamboo so as it could be used within the zoo for replanting, or for elephant food. Being somewhat bored out of my mind with the repetitious sweeping and cleaning duties, I somehow managed to make an uninvited place for myself in the van, and although they were surprised, strangely enough no one questioned me, and they all accepted that I had been requested to go. I had an enjoyable day working with the staff that were impressed with my input. I would sometimes be found with the wife of one of the curators tending to the baby otters in one of the off-limit areas. The zoo also had a substantial animal nursery where visitors could enter the world of Baby Animals and watch them being cared for via large glass viewing windows. There was also a circular enclosure, outside the nursery that housed a variety of young animals, even a young bear at one time. I worked within the zoo over a period of three years and during my last year a close friend of mine also gained a position with me. Little did I know then that this was the very beginning of my eventual pathway to working at the zoo as a keeper.

I eventually completed and obtained my Higher School Certificate and worked for a short while at a local pie shop in High St Preston. I learnt quite a bit about the trade along the way working very long hours and learning how to make pies, pasties, sausage rolls and a myriad of other pastries. I worked there longer than I expected to, for a very low wage. I would finish at times late at night after starting at dawn. It gave me some valuable experience in working with a team although at times I felt that I was the only one designated to do the dirty work such as cleaning the walk-through passage way adjacent to the shop where customers could view the art of pie making through a series of windows.

I worked there for several years before eventually leaving to look for something more rewarding and substantial.

CHAPTER 4

Into the Work Force

So with my Higher School certificate under my arm I ventured into the world of the unemployed, looking at the weekly newspaper's positions vacant section and marching into the city to apply or to sit with sometimes hundreds of other applicants in large offices to complete an aptitude test, knowing that jobs were few and far between at the time and companies could employ desperate job seekers that were overqualified for the position or positions available. After many weeks of trudging through the city streets I decided to approach it from a different angle and walked into a dingy employment office to see what was available. As luck would have it a vacant position was available in Richmond at a Repco Part store outlet, working in the delivery department. So after making a phone call and making my way to the location, it didn't take much after being shown around by the foreman at the factory to inform me that the job was mine if I wanted it, which made me wonder how many other people had previously turned it down as it was very basic position and looked like I was in for some hard work in not such pleasant surroundings. So I presented myself as their new full-time store boy on the following Monday morning.

The following six months entailed toil and hard work, taking iron rods and other metal and plastic products off the back of trucks, for the machines in the factory to turn them into contact sets or distributor caps for cars. My hands and arms would ache at night from all the heavy lifting and sorting, but after some time I was transferred to the parts store to fill in orders from the factory to distribute parts to the machines, which was less physically demanding. After several months I was offered a position in the office processing work orders. Just as I was beginning to enjoy the office environs and the people I was working with, I was informed by management that due to unforeseen circumstances they would have to let me go as the company was in some financial trouble, confirming all the rumours which had been floating around. Possibly feeling sorry for me he gave me a week off with pay to enable me to find another position elsewhere. As luck would have it several days later my sister informed me that CIG, The Commonwealth Industrial Gases, in Preston, was looking for a Petty Cash Clerk and within a few days of being interviewed I had a new job, thanks no doubt to my sister and my previous office experience at Repco and a good reference from them.

I spent just on twelve years at CIG working my way through various departments, such as accounts payable and eventually as a contracts officer, making many friends along the way, many of whom I still see today. Even though I was very happy where I was, I knew all along that my passion was to work in the zoo in the field of animal husbandry. I later joined Friends of the Zoo which was officially launched in 1980. Some years later it had reached 100,000 members, quite an achievement as at that time, the Collingwood Football Club only had something like 70,000 members! Sometime later I joined the first group, fourteen people in all, led by the zoo's zoologist to be trained as zoo guides. After an extensive training program each person selected an animal within the zoo's collection to do a presentation on, as part of their graduation process. This was conducted in the presence of the rest of the group. Mine was the hippopotamus. One of the behaviours of hippos is that as they defecate they scatter their faeces by flicking their tail. This is a way of marking their territory and communicating with other hippos and is overall a display of dominance. Just as I was informing my fellow zoo guides, the hippo, as if on call, did just that.

After a number of months we all successfully graduated and were presented with our Zoo Guiding Certificates by Alfred Dunbavin Butcher, the zoo's Chairman of the Board. So here I was, one of the certified Zoo Guides eager to impart my knowledge of the animals within Melbourne Zoo, and I regularly made myself available on most weekends and public holidays. Friends of the Zoo also had fundraising activities for new enclosures and promoted animal sponsorship. I even expanded my activities outside of the zoo walls by putting together a display within the front window of the Preston library. But even with all this, when all was said and done I knew that I wanted more of a permanent connection with the zoo in the form of full-time employment as a keeper.

Now the usual process to apply for a keeping position within the zoo at that time was to send an application of interest to the then director every year. I however had other ideas and began applying every six months or so, and when I was in the zoo conducting guided tours would let senior and other staff members know of my zoo employment intentions.

I would also visit, as I had as a kid, the local aquarium not far from home, where I would frequently help out doing water changes, or decorating aquariums, and I was always passionate and keen to do whatever I could to help out. The proprietor was rather a rough-and-ready individual, but he could be pleasant for some of the time. He was however also lazy, and he got lazier as I took on more tasks and it came down to me to attending to the tanks more than I should have to. One day while he was serving a customer he blasted me for some reason or another maybe showing off. As I had done nothing to deserve this reaction from him I placed a hose in a tank that didn't contain fish, turned it on full blast, and walked out of the shop. I wasn't going to allow him to treat me in such a manner for my free services. I heard later he wanted to contact me to have me back, but I made no effort to contact him. It was at this time I began getting involved and seriously interested in the wonderful world of fish keeping, setting up numerous aquariums at home housing many varieties of South American fish.

A retail aquarium I frequented operated and owned by an older experienced aquarist, who would import vast quantities of fish from South America and other parts of the world. It was indeed interesting to discuss fish issues with him over a coffee. As he imported so many fish that were sought after by many aquarists he was always on the go but still had time for us. Some of his sales tanks were on an angle due to the fact that the floor was becoming rather unstable and all you had to do was to place your hand on the surface of the water to have so many fish appear from the depths of the murky water eager to feed. There would always be several armies of ants that had made their homes within the many gaps and crevices in the tank stands. Some cracks that appeared on the edges of some of his sales tanks were just taped up with just sticky tape. It wasn't the appearance of the shop that concerned the proprietor, it was what was in them that was counted. I believe he enjoyed the company of the ants and other insects that made their home within the crevices, cracks and holes in his shop. He would at times have numerous cardboard boxes full of screaming young Sulphur-crested Cockatoos on makeshift benches eager to be fed just like the fish, and would make a handsome profit from their sales. One day over a coffee a woman came into the shop. Now the shop itself was not what you would call clean and organised. There were equipment shipment boxes, dirt and dust everywhere, including the glass display units. The woman, noticing this, made comment as to the dirty dark state of the shop, upon which the proprietor quickly informed her that diamonds are found in dirty dusty areas such as his, indicating the rare fish species he sold. She didn't get it at all and thundered out of the shop with her daughter in tow. Another time he told off a customer who had referred to some of his aquatic plants as weeds, and on wishing to purchase some of his aquatic plants he complained that he had to get his arms wet to serve such a rude and ignorant customer who just wanted to buy some aquatic weeds.

He was never backwards in coming forwards and always spoke his mind. I purchased many rare fish from him and enjoyed visits to his aquarium over many years, he is long gone now, maybe in that dirty dusty aquarium in the sky.

I continued to collect many species of fish and had an offer to breed some species for a local aquarium but decided against it as I just wanted to maintain keeping fish as a hobby for enjoyment.

After some two years of sending my letters of interest to Melbourne Zoo, the day finally arrived when I received a letter to make an appointment to come into the zoo for an interview, as a keeping position had become available within the Native Mammal department. At last I knew I had the opportunity to achieve my ultimate goal.

On the day of the interview I was directed into the Curatorial office where I was greeted by the Curators, some who recognised me from my Guiding duties and zoo visitations. The interview went well, and my responses to the questions were acknowledged favourably, as I wanted to show my passion for securing a keeping position. With the process completed I was approached by one of the Head Curators to inform me that my interview had been rated highly, and I was in a very good position to secure the vacancy. There was however one more applicant to be interviewed, and I would be informed of the outcome later that day, but as it stood I was the favoured candidate. I was in awe of all this feedback and believed I had a high chance of being the successful applicant. Some considerable time passed that day as I sat in the office anxiously waiting on the imminent phone call, wading through endless paperwork. When the expected call did come through I was informed that I had missed out by the narrowest of margins, and as the final applicant had had experience with captive possums and he had been given the position. I was shattered to have come so close and yet missed out. After several weeks of coming to terms with the reality of it all, I become more reflective of my situation and was determined for this set back not to hinder my overall goal. If experience is what I needed I was determined to get just that.

CHAPTER 5

Reptile and Fauna Reserve

So in those days how did one find such an opportunity to gain experience in working with animals apart from a zoo? Well, believe it or not, I found it in the Yellow Pages Telephone Directory under 'Z' for zoos of course. And there it was, Reptile and Fauna Reserve. I was aware of one of the owners who appeared at that time on a variety of television shows with various animals from the reserve. One being *Shirl's Neighbourhood* which was a children's television series, first aired on the seven network and was hosted by the late Shirley Strachan, and *The Early Bird Breakfast Show* was aired on Channel Ten at the time and featured Marty the Monster and his female hostess. Reptile and Fauna Reserve was purchased by the two owners in 1979 and opened to the public in 1980. So after contacting them and making an appointment, I made the one-hour drive and upon arriving I introduced myself and explained my intentions of gaining animal husbandry experience. At first they informed me that they did not take on volunteers, however due to the fact that I wished to use the experience to gain a keeping position at Melbourne Zoo and my involvement as a Zoo Guide, they made an exception and took me on. So I felt as if I had one big toe in the door and was elated they had taken a chance with me, and I had no intention of letting them down.

The very next weekend I arrived for my first day eager to prove myself. My first task was to rake several large kangaroo paddocks, some that looked like they had never seen a rake before, but I took to the task with a smile on my face and after some 40 minutes or so, the owners with rakes in hand joined me, wondering what they had been possibly missing out on. One of my first animal encounters was with the resident wombat and as I entered the enclosure to clean, the wombat was in his burrow which could be viewed through a glass window. After a while he appeared and was not impressed with my presence as he stood in front of me. I proceeded to finish the task at hand and left him to his solitude, only to be informed later by the owners that they always locked him in his off-limit area when cleaning, due to his highly aggressive nature. Maybe it was because I stood my ground that bluffed him.

The reserve housed a large collection of native mammals, such as Red and Grey Kangaroos, dingoes, possums, reptiles, and several pumas. It didn't take me long to settle into the routine, arriving early each morning to feed baby wombats or 'roos and go about the task of cleaning exhibits and the surrounds. I had several close calls. One with Rags, a huge male Red Kangaroo which the owners would take into television studios where Rags, as he was called, would often come to grips with the hosts, on one occasion Rags attacking Marty the Monster, a fellow in a large furry costume, who had become a popular morning show character. If it wasn't for the heavy duty costume the wearer could have received very serious injuries. Rags not only had him in a full grip at the time but also had him on the ground. The owner had been warned by us as to the danger of this, but decided to go ahead with it anyway, after all as it was good publicity. The following week an adult African python was taken in which resulted in the snake biting the fur of Marty the Monster's costume. Some weeks later while I was cleaning Rag's paddock he managed to get into the same area with me, and on hearing him directly behind me ready to do some kind of mischief with me. It's quite amazing how, in never being all that athletic I still managed to clear the fence in one swift desperate leap.

One of the most popular presentations that the owners would conduct was the Snakes Alive show where they would put on very informative Reptile Shows in many schools and shopping centres within Victoria. These proved to be most popular and every year their mailbox would be bulging, full of show requests. It proved to be a financial boon for the owners and the shows were beneficial in educating school children and the general public about reptiles. Later on the owners made animals available for various film companies and shows that again boosted the park's coffers and popularity.

The income from these events assisted with the expense of building or improving enclosures and I would find myself working alongside the owners completing such tasks. One friend of the owners arranged for two of his dingoes to be looked after while he was away interstate, however he failed to return leaving his dingoes with a new permanent home with us.

So it was necessary to increase the size of the enclosure, resulting in an area much more spacious and comfortable. Mundane tasks such as cleaning the rat and mouse breeding facility and cleaning the Reptile House were given to me to test me out, but I took on the tasks as I had as a kid working at the zoo, minus standing around just looking at the animals. I also got the chance on numerous occasions to walk the resident dingoes along the adjoining river. I was rewarded one day in foiling an attempted theft of a Shingleback Lizard from the Reptile House with the thief being a visitor from overseas caught red-handed by yours truly as he attempted to conceal the reptile in the pocket of his overcoat.

All ran smoothly within the park and weekends would be filled with visitors enjoying the surrounds and demonstrations that we would deliver, sometimes one of the owner's parents came in to lend a hand on Public Holidays when the crowds would swell. They were good times that I relished and was constantly recognised for my input and efforts. One day I arrived to see the local handyman who was employed by the owners from time to time, constructing some brick dens and marking out an area to be fenced off. This was to be a new lion enclosure with room to accommodate another species of big cat. Several months later a female lion was transported to the park, she was in the very early stages of pregnancy. The lion in question was acquired from the Bacchus Marsh Lion Park.

Several weeks later I was made aware that the other area next to the lions was to accommodate a tiger. The following weekend one of the owners and myself drove the two hours to the Bacchus Marsh Lion Park to take delivery of it.

Bacchus Marsh Lion Safari was opened in 1970 and closed in 1985; the year I started my career at the zoo. The park covered ten acres, and the public were able to drive into the large fenced off enclosures to have close up lion and tiger encounters, from within the safety of their vehicles. In 1972 a lioness gave birth to four cubs, the first time a litter of lion cub quads were born in Australia. In 1979 a keeper was clawed by a tiger, and a 30-year-old woman was mauled by a tiger when she opened the window of her car. In the same year a 12-year-old boy was attacked and killed by a lion. The boy's father was working on some nearby dens at the time of the incident. There seemed to be a decision not to investigate further. Eventually the park was closed down, with some animals being relocated to other zoos.

When we arrived at the Safari Park it became immediately obvious that the park was in a state of decline. The remaining lions in the park were housed in a large circular enclosure. With only some corrugated iron dens for shelter, and several half barrels of water, there were no off-limit areas or access points to the enclosure. Hence I now knew where the building materials had come from to build the lion enclosure back at the reserve, as there were large quantities of Cyclone fencing and other materials lying around that had come from the decommissioned enclosures. The tigers were held in a rectangular cage, one male and one female. The male Karliff was destined for us. The enclosure was rather unkempt, and the tigers were pacing from one end to the other, sensing that something was about to happen, which indeed it was. Karliff had been used to promote Bata School Shoes and appeared in a number of television advertisements. The soles of the shoes had tiger prints, apparently taken from Karliff's paw prints, so children wearing them would leave tiger paw tracks. Karliff was also raised and cared for by two keepers who I later worked with at Melbourne Zoo.

The vehicle we had chosen to transport Karliff was a Ford F100 covered truck, no transport box, just the back area to contain the tiger. We had secured a heavy-duty Cyclone panel at the back of the seats to protect and keep us separated from Karliff. It took some time to back the truck up to a section of the enclosure so a panel could be removed and pulled aside to give Karliff full access to the back of the truck. We had no other way of doing this, and after some anxious and what could be considered dangerous moments, we eventually managed to entice him inside the vehicle. By this time Karliff was extremely agitated, pacing and vocalising, while attempting to find an escape route. We gave him some time to settle down before our return journey. It was a long stressful return trip not only for us but for Karliff, with lots of tiger phlegm on the back of our necks. Upon arrival back at the park we eventually managed to get him into his new home without incident and I was relieved that he was at that time in a larger and better place. It was from this time on, after this tiger acquisition, that things began to significantly change.

With lions and a tiger on the premises it didn't take too long for the phone to start running hot at night or in the morning with complaints from local residents about the nocturnal roaring. This eventually led to some pretty threatening calls, letters and sometimes messages stuck on the perimeter fences. Some were concerned that there would be an escapee. We would invite the locals to have a look around to assure them that everything was safe and secure and of course to bring their families along free of charge. Other residents felt that it was pretty cool to hear lions and tigers so close to where they lived.

Part of the deal for the tiger and lion acquisition was, I believe, for ex lion park hands to be able to take up residency in caravans within the reserve. Some no doubt had worked on the road with the circus or worked at the lion park at some time. The part they were to play was not made all that clear to me, but it became obvious that none of them were willing to do any work, even if that was the intention. The only things that began to appear were piles of empty alcohol bottles and cans outside their caravans making the place look unsightly and untidy. Time and time again I would find myself knocking on caravan doors, sometimes early in the morning to attempt to get some response to get them to earn their keep, or at least to make an effort to remove the piles of bottles that got higher every day. Over time the areas around the caravans became unsightly, and I became fearful that things would progressively get worse. Even visitors were becoming aware of the situation and would comment on it. These so-called workers did little to convince me that they had any intention of working at all, although some made an effort to hold a rake to make themselves look busy, but it didn't fool me.

One busy weekend I was instructed to hose the female lion from her den, in order to separate her from her cubs, and take her two lion cubs up to the main entrance for the visitors to hold and have photos taken with them, at a cost of course. I flatly refused and stood my ground, not because I had not been told by one of the owners, but because it was unethical and cruel. I received some verbal rebuff from my refusal, but I was determined that I was not going to accommodate these demands. However apart from all that was happening, the reptiles that had been housed in a large room connected to the house were moved to a new reptile house facility that was a huge improvement.

Several months later the reserve acquired a Black Leopard and several other animals from a park in Northern Victoria only to be placed in makeshift enclosures with the intention of expanding them in the future, which never eventuated. I made it clear that these makeshift enclosures were not in my mind adequate for the animals they housed. Some circus hands believed that it was safe enough to venture in with some carnivores and do feeding sessions, which was just plain dangerous. One of the owners was away most of the time travelling to various film locations providing kangaroos, wombats and various reptiles for television shows and productions.

This situation just left me and the other owner to carry out all or most of the general husbandry duties around the grounds and for me to constantly be told by the outside influences as to what to do and not to do.

It was eventually sold in the 1990s.

CHAPTER 6

The Zoo at Last

Just as I was giving serious consideration to leaving Reptile and Fauna Reserve, a letter from Melbourne Zoo arrived inviting me to attend an interview for a keeping position which had become available within the reptile department. So with a chance to get away from all that was happening and with a great well-earned reference under my arm, I presented myself to be interviewed at the zoo's Curator's Office. Once again I felt confident as I went through the process, feeling that I had presented myself well with some raised eyebrows re the animal husbandry experience I had gained at Reptile and Fauna Reserve. The call came later that day from the Curator of reptiles, informing me that I was the successful applicant. At last after some three years of frustration and hard work I had accomplished what I had set out to achieve. So in looking back Reptile and Fauna Reserve was the vehicle I had needed to gain experience to set me up for a keeping career at the zoo. And I will always remain thankful to the owners that they took a chance with me and gave me the opportunity to gain valuable experience to set myself up for a zookeeping career.

So after all that I had gone through there was one more task before I could feel completely comfortable in taking on my new career path, and that was informing my father. My Dad and I got on very well and I knew deep down inside he was pleased that I was working in an office at CIG. He was well regarded and respected at Dalgety & Co and was responsible for major implementations in the company. So I took it upon myself to visit him and give him the news. He sat quietly and listened to what I had to say knowing that he was well aware of my vast interest in the natural world. He then congratulated me and understood that this was what I had always wanted. Dad would visit me from time to time at work over the years and was always fascinated by what I was doing and involved in, and was always as enthusiastic as I was. I know that he was proud of what I had achieved and was always encouraging in my career pursuits.

CHAPTER 7

The House of Reptiles

Many, many years before in the early 1900s the Reptile House was located in a different area from where it currently stands. As heating was not provided in this facility many reptiles did not thrive and there was a high mortality rate in the colder months. The story in those days is one that when snakes arrived at the zoo in boxes lined with blankets it was proposed that such items could be provided for the snakes as a source of warmth during the cold winter months. On discovering the disappearance of a blanket it was assumed that one of the pythons had consumed it mistaking it for a meal. As this story was conveyed by a minister's wife and other factors one would have serious doubts about such a story.

It was January 1985 when I stepped into Melbourne Zoo, as the newest member of the keeping team. Much had changed since my school zoo working days. Almost 200 animals had been born at the zoo and the Butterfly House was opened, being the first of its kind in the Southern Hemisphere and in 1990 the enclosure was dedicated to Dr Alfred Dunbavin Butcher who was the main instigator of the exhibit. He was a Melbourne Zoo Board Member from 1947 until 1987 including 20 years as Chairman. Also some 220,000 Students had visited Zoos Victoria Education Department that year.

I was shown around the property and the Reptile House by the keeper I was replacing, leaving me in awe of the size of the collection. The public viewing area alone consisted of 31 displays and numerous reptile holding facilities in the off-limit areas. The circular building still stands today and had been a holding area for rhesus monkeys many years ago. It was refurbished and reopened as a Reptile House in 1969. Displays varied from large, small and medium and could be serviced from the front sliding lockable windows, each unit had an artificial rock wall escarpment made from wire mesh and concrete with cement colouring to give it a natural appearance. The keeper in charge of birds and reptiles developed this effect and he also did some major work in applying this in the small cat enclosures. The small enclosures had solid domestic shower bases, that could if needed hold water and could be emptied from the rear of each display. Each unit represented the natural environment of the species exhibited, around Australia and the world. I soon fell into the routine of servicing and feeding not to mention all the other demanding tasks that one had to perform, this took me some time to get my head around and that I was willing to learn and commit myself to the set tasks demanded of me. There were times I felt that I was only spoken to when I was asked to do something or had forgotten to do it. Maybe I was just being put to the test. There were so many other tasks apart from servicing the exhibits, such as looking after the live crickets, grasshoppers, mealworms, and rats and mice. It was always a full busy daily schedule as there were only two of us on the department, and many times I was left to my own devices if the Head Keeper had meetings and other issues to attend to. We worked alternate weekends solo, and it would involve just the standard basic routine and duties, and other additional tasks would be carried out during the week when we were both rostered on. As the Reptile House didn't open until around 10am we had just two hours to clean and service all of the displays. There were several outdoor lizard enclosures that had to be attended to later in the day, as well as feeding the invertebrates and the live rat and mice colonies all used as food for the resident reptiles. Once the public gallery was cleaned and opened there were also two other large off-limit areas that contained reptiles that were surplus to the collection, or under medication, and others some requiring special attention. There was also a kitchen that connected to a service causeway that accommodated a desk for doing paperwork, keeping records and some fish tanks containing various reptiles as well as a rat and mice facility. Every reptile had an identification record card that would show when it had last been fed and how much it had fed, as well as when it had last shed its skin, or if it had been treated or was under treatment for some particular issue. Every inch of the off-limit areas was full to capacity. Everything was operated to a high standard, with no exceptions. Working solo was at times a lonely experience, and it was always a welcome relief if someone came down to join you for a cuppa, or I would head up to other departments at breaks.

The workday ran from 8am in the morning till 5pm, with a 5.30pm finish on weekends and Public Holidays. The roster at the time would have us working some twelve days straight and work every second weekend. There were times that I wondered what I had got myself into as this was the pinnacle of the trade and it demanded much from me, yet I persisted and eventually fell into the routine.

On one wall as you entered the office area was what we named the Horror Wall, showing real life colour photos of what damage reptiles are capable of inflicting upon us. An image of a huge Asian python cut open to reveal a child that had been consumed, whole of course. Another of a young boy with his leg on a chair showing his shin bone, revealing massive tissue damage due to the effects of a viper bite being left untreated. There were other images depicting gory photos of the results of reptile encounters. Visitors and other keepers were always fascinated by them. To us I believe it was a great permanent reminder of what could happen. Some years later, some 48 tiered-holding units were installed to allow us to properly manage the increase of reptile numbers, including our off-limit collection. All the units had individual thermostatically controlled heating units, which proved to be very time efficient and made maximum use of the available space. As this new facility proved to be very successful the back wall of the Reptile House was removed and extended into a much larger and more spacious working area.

The Reptile House still stands today as an excellent example of what can be achieved from a building that once just held monkeys.

The Grey Ghost

Our Curator of Reptiles at the time was affectionately called the Grey Ghost, as he had the ability to walk up behind you without being heard. He caught me and other staff members off guard on several occasions. One was as I was feeding the giant tree frogs on display one morning with a colleague, he approached us undetected and upon uttering a "good morning" directly behind us, frogs, crickets and feeding forceps went sailing into the air in all directions. Another time as I was leaving the Reptile House late one winter's night, he was standing at the main door. He appeared before me from nowhere, resulting in my feet totally leaving the ground in sheer fright.

During the winter months he would bring down some seedlings and place them high up on a shelf in the off-limits of reptiles so they could get the sun and warmth, giving them a head start for spring. He asked me one day if I could tend to them as he was going on leave for a few days. On getting up to the shelf the following morning I was confronted by several plastic dinosaurs, placed there to give me a fright, which I might add they failed to do. Upon his return he was greeted by a larger dinosaur and as time went on so did this tit for tat. One day while shopping with my son who was also into dinosaurs at the time, we came across an enormous plastic beast of a dinosaur, the biggest I had ever seen. In informing my son that I would purchase this for him, in exchange him allowing to me to use it for the tit for tat prank to which he agreed. I had not seen my intended victim for some time and was beginning to think that maybe he had removed his seedlings, but several days later the Reptile House was filled with a blood-curdling scream, confirming that my latest purchase had been discovered, and I knew that I had won that tit for tat competition.

The Curator of Reptiles lived on the premises opposite the food store. He had within his back garden an impressive collection of birds and reptiles, which he asked me to look after while he was away on leave. It wasn't until I ventured into his garden that I became aware just how massive this menagerie was. Over the week he was away I had to spend a serious amount of time feeding and cleaning the birds and reptiles in his collection.

When he eventually retired and left the zoo all of the keeping staff formed an avenue of honour as he departed through the zoo gates for the last time.

Iggy and Strop

One of the iconic lizards in the collection was Iggy the Rhinoceros Iguana. These lizards grow to a considerable size, they are a species found in the Caribbean Islands of Hispaniola and its surrounding islands. They vary in length from 60 to 136 cm and are a steel-grey colour with a somewhat prehistoric appearance. Iggy had been in the collection for a long time. When cleaning his exhibit he was allowed to roam the Reptile House at will. Sometimes taking advantage of having access to the off-limit areas where at times we would let him stay during the day to have a change of scenery. When he was hungry, which was most of the time, he would dive into his large food tray scattering most of the contents everywhere except in his mouth. He would also come up behind you to grab your boot or ankle to remind you that he was hungry. One morning while he was exploring an off-limit area he sat at the base of a ladder where one of the electricians was working, only to greet him with an open mouth when the electrician descended, the house was filled with blood-curdling screams.

Iggy was most of the time very obliging and would allow you to pick him up, where he would sit along your arm. He would always be introduced to visitors, some from overseas, where he sat calmly on my arm. However on one occasion while he was resting on me in his usual position, he bit the keeper that pointed out his mouth and then defecated all down my front. When Iggy passed away we had a funeral service inviting all the staff to attend. Iggy, after visiting a taxidermist, was used as an exhibit for students in the Keeper Education Department. He was the last of his kind until others were obtained many years later.

The other resident of the house was Strop, a Blue-tongued Lizard that lived under the fridge in the kitchen. Most people I am sure are familiar with this lizard, found around residential gardens from time to time. Strop would often almost be stood on when he scurried across the floor, or he would suddenly appear when he wanted to be fed. He would always hiss at you hence his name. One day for no apparent reason he ate a piece of plastic which proved to be his last meal. We had a morning tea funeral service for him as we did for Iggy. I will always have fond memories of these two iconic lizards that once shared our working day.

Auntie and Oscar

Saltwater Crocodiles are the largest of the living reptiles and can grow up to 6 meters in length with the females being considerably smaller. They are opportunistic and are considered to be the apex predator. They will prey on almost any animal that ventures into their territory, including us.

Auntie and Oscar, our two large crocodiles, occupied the largest exhibit area within the Reptile House, which also housed a large pool for them to swim in. The exhibit could be divided in two by a large steel sliding gate. This gate would come into good use if we had to separate the female Auntie if she was gravid, that is due to lay eggs, or if Oscar got too aggressive towards her, as he was much larger and was capable of inflicting an injury, she could then be safely separated.

It was on this occasion that they were separated as Auntie was due to lay eggs which we would collect and incubate ourselves. This required two keepers, one to lasso Auntie around her snout and pull her into a large ditch parallel to the viewing window, upon which a board was placed over the ditch, and for one of the keepers to stand on it while the other would venture into the nest area to collect the eggs and place them carefully into a bucket. One day after Auntie had deposited her eggs, I was the nominated Bucket Boy Egg Collector. After I carefully removed the eggs and handing the egg-laden bucket to the Curator of Reptiles, who was assisting me at the time, he then stepped out, leaving a very angry Auntie half out of the pit facing me for a standoff. I wasn't up for that challenge and launched myself over her and into the viewing area via the gap in the window, once more proving that I had great jumping abilities as I had performed when Rags confronted me. I was horrified that the Curator had done this without any regard for my safety and went about his business as if it had not happened at all. Was it a test of my resolve? I will never know but I knew that next season I wouldn't be the bucket boy.

I had two other episodes, both with Oscar. The first was when I was training a new keeper who had come onto the department from another division. During the morning clean Oscar was due to be fed, this involved partially opening the large sliding window while Oscar waited for his breakfast. He would always launch himself from the water and broadside the window, not too hard but just enough to put the willies up you. But this time instead of broadsiding, he hit the window full on nose first, which resulted in a considerable hole smashed in the middle of the window. He sat back in the water with a slight trickle of blood on his nose, as surprised as we were. I managed to get him to the other side of the dividing gate and secured him and the window and then placed a barrier tape to prevent any visitors from venturing too close. Later on that day, a glazier, while replacing the sliding window, informed me that the glass was not toughened, or shatter proof! Go figure.

One chore I detested most was during summer all the Perspex sheets, which during winter sat between the roof battens supported by chicken wire acting as heat insulators, had to be removed, cleaned, dried and returned. This involved pulling the Perspex sheets along behind you while crawling along the narrow roof space. As the roof was corrugated iron it got very hot within the cramped space. Once dried and cleaned, we then had to repeat the process crawling back into the roof, which resulted in cuts, scratches and bruising along the way, not to mention a feeling of total exhaustion and heat stroke. Oscar loved this time of year as he would cruise in the water below you, then launch himself vertically out of the water and snap at you. You always knew he could not possibly reach you at that height, but he gave it a good go. The next year one of our new younger keepers got the opportunity to carry out this task, I can still see his sheer white face to this day after completing the task. It was the last time I ever crawled into the roof space of the Reptile House and would never envy anyone who would have to perform it.

Gone in a Flash Part 1

Working solo one morning after emptying out one of the python ponds, I went to get the hose to refill it, on my return finding that the resident python had mysteriously vanished. I quickly checked every corner of the display and the immediate area, but no sign of him anywhere. As I was moving out of the display there he was back in the pond. How did he do that? I then turned to pick up the hose and he had disappeared again. Scratching my head in absolute amazement I looked around to see if someone was pulling a prank on me. As no one was around I quickly discounted that possibility. I then once again explored the immediate surrounds and then the pythons head appeared from a hole in the side of the pond, just big enough for him to crawl in and out of. The hole was later filled in, much to the displeasure of the python.

One of my very first feeding jobs was when cleaning an off-display tank containing three Red Bellied Black Snakes. It was the common procedure to separate them, and then allow them to feed, prior to putting them back together again. Although I had done this before at Reptile and Fauna Reserve, and with the Head Keeper in the same room at his desk watching out of the corner of his eye no doubt at my technique, I made an error, allowing one of the Red Bellies to consume one of the smaller ones, leaving us with only two. Looking back at it today the three snakes should not have been together in the first place, as even after putting them back together after feeding the scent of the mice on them could result in cannibalistic behaviour. Maybe I should have pointed this out at the time, but it was too late, and I could almost feel his look of disapproval burning the back of my neck. I eventually stopped punishing myself and put it down to experience.

Gone in a Flash Part 2

We had recently placed several Sail-Finned Philippine Lizards on display. They had been in quarantine after being transported from overseas, they are fast moving and grow to around 106 cm. They are quite a spectacular lizard and as per their name have large sail-like fins along their backs, giving them a prehistoric appearance. They can grow to a considerable size reaching some 91 cm to 120 cm and can weigh as much as two kilograms. On this particular weekend morning, while servicing the display, one of them managed to scuttle under the glass sliding door and into the then empty viewing gallery just as the door was closing. So here I was in a reverse situation with him on the outside and me on the inside, leaving me looking through the closed window from within the exhibit at the lizard on the viewing visitor gallery floor and within seconds he tilted his head in my direction, then disappeared at lightning speed. So this left me in a dilemma, do I attempt to chase after it, or hope it turns up sometime during the day? I went for the latter as I still had heaps of work ahead of me before I opened the reptile house. So for the rest of the day I was on the lookout for the escapee. Later that afternoon while working in the centre off-limit area, I happened to spot my escapee. It was sitting in a difficult high position and was distracted by something, so it was not aware of me. I had but one chance as I got myself into position, one that required me to launch myself at it from behind. Memories of my leaping abilities re Rags and Auntie came flashing back. As luck would have it I managed to do just that, launching myself far enough and grabbing it at the lower part of its body just below the back legs which enabled it to turn around and bite me. With blood streaming from my hand I yelled, not from the pain of the bite, but in sheer delight at my rewarding brilliant catch that would put me into serious contention for a position on any cricket team. And to top it off no one would be the wiser. It was then that I noticed from the corner of my eye that many eyes were upon me from the other side of the off-limit area. Undetected by me as I stalked my prey a Zoo Guide group had entered the area escorted by one of the head keepers, who sometime later approached me regarding the incident. After all, how could he be annoyed as I had just demonstrated a perfect example of capture and restraint?

There were several other escapes that are worthy of a mention, one being a Western Brown Snake that managed to exit its display via an undetected hole at the very rear of its abode. We of course frantically searched in vain for this very venomous snake, but to no avail and after some time we decided to report the incident. As we both looked at one another with worried looks there was a knock on the door with an elderly visitor informing us that a brown-coloured snake had been seen near the pathway leading to the reptile house. In a mad rush we almost knocked the poor woman over and within minutes we arrived at the area of the sighting and as luck would have it managed to capture the snake without too much trouble, only to inform the onlookers that it was indeed harmless. A lie worth telling to prevent any panic, and relief in not having to report the incident.

Another day we found that there was only one Corn Snake in the off-limit holding unit when there should have been two, it later turned up under a bin lid outside the back door. Corn Snakes are not venomous and are relatively harmless, still it was a relief once again all the same.

On crawling through the Reptile House roof cavity one of the electricians came across the remains of a discarded snakeskin of a python, resulting in him making a very quick exit. As all the pythons within the collection were present and accounted for, it's remained a mystery even to this day.

Wilbur

Wilbur is an Aldabran Giant Tortoise who still resides at the zoo, and is the oldest and largest in the zoo, hatching sometime around 1930 and is quite capable of living to 150 years of age, which possibly means he can live until 2080! Aldabran Tortoises are only second in size to the Galapagos Tortoises, able to reach a weight of some 181 kg and a length of 1.219 metres. They are endemic to the Aldabra Atoll Seychelles, an archipelago nation off the coast of Africa. The giant tortoises resided at the zoo then in a considerably large area where they had access to their night den, which is heated over the winter months. When in his enclosure Wilbur had a habit of coming up behind you, raising himself as high as he could, and then falling forward to hit you solidly on the back of your legs with the top section of his shell. He would also, if he got the opportunity, attempt to bite you, which would result in considerable damage. I had only just warned a volunteer keeper of this behaviour when he was struck from behind, sending him crashing to the ground, fortunately with nothing broken, but Wilbur looking rather proud of himself at his achievement. The area where he still resides with his females has been greatly increased giving them much more room to roam in.

A Reticulated Move

We had two Reticulated Pythons within one of the large enclosures, a male and female. Reticulated Pythons have attractive markings, with a black oblong circular pattern with yellow, white and grey colours entwined within. They are the largest species of pythons from southeast Asia and can grow to some 4.8 meters or more and have been recorded at a weight of 170 kg. They are a species known to have a very aggressive nature and we would always be aware of where they were when we cleaned their enclosure and kept a considerable distance from them. One keeper was bitten on the face by the male but was fortunately able to move far enough away to only sustain bruising to his face. They were always at their most dangerous at feeding time, where they would move towards you in a hungry, menacing way. Dead rabbits would be offered on long, solid feeding tongs, and as they would coil around the rabbit that would often include the tongs, so we would have to wait for the rabbit to be consumed before we could retrieve them.

The male had been moved into a large rectangular fibreglass container as he had been having difficulty shedding or sloughing his skin as all snakes do from time to time as they grow. He was in shallow warm water to assist with the shedding process and most of the skin had come away and we needed to place him back into his enclosure. This of course needed to be performed before the Reptile House was to open and required quite a number of staff members to assist. One or two people to hold the head, which was a huge task in itself, while about six others held the body to prevent the python from coiling them up and reversing the situation. One person was also required to keep the female in the enclosure and at bay as well. It was the first time many of us had performed such a task and the sheer strength of the snake was incredible. After much pushing, yelling, grunting and straining we managed to get him back where he belonged, hoping and praying that his next shed would be a clean one, and would not require our intervention.

A Haul in a Suitcase

In my first year on reptiles Custom Officers intercepted a German tourist at Melbourne Airport with 63 lizards, mainly blue tongues and shinglebacks, in a suitcase destined for his homeland. He was rather alarmed to learn that exporting native animals was illegal. He believed that because the lizards in question were not endangered that they could be taken out of the country. The smuggler had caught the lizards at Port Augusta and near Broken Hill. They all arrived OK at the Reptile House, where they were all checked re their health and apart from a few mites and ticks were deemed healthy. The German visitor had been to Australia seven times before and admitted that he had previously taken some twenty-five reptiles out of the country. He was released on bail with a $10,000 surety and was to appear later in court. We never heard the outcome of the court case, but we hoped that he had learnt his lesson and would not reoffend. The lizards remained in our collection, some of them going to the animal section in the education department. I wondered if he was the individual that I caught attempting to steal one of the lizards at Reptile and Fauna Reserve.

In other cases Wildlife Departments would confiscate reptiles from residents who did not have a licence. They were mainly python species, and soon our off-limit collection and work demand increased. Some had to be held until a licence could be applied for and issued. This meant that we were actually looking after peoples snakes free of charge. So after almost running out of space to house them, we suggested that if the set up to house these pythons was up to scratch, why not leave them with the owner, fine them, and then issue them with the licence. Otherwise they would need to set up a facility at the zoo to house the confiscations. They wisely opted for the first option which eliminated a lot of workload from us.

Monitor Mayhem

One of the other duties on the Reptile Round was to service a large oval-shaped lace monitor enclosure. It was located at the other end of the zoo near the native mammal section, containing four aggressive occupants which would rush at the door in anticipation as you entered with a bucket full of rats, and a broom. As the enclosure was very old it did not have an airlock attached to it. An airlock is a cage that you enter, lock and secure, before opening the main door to the enclosure, ensuring that the occupants within cannot get past you and escape. This enclosure not only didn't have an airlock, but a very low single-entry door that you had to bend down to get through. With four hungry lizards rushing the door you only had a matter of seconds to fend them off. This not only placed you in a very dangerous situation, but could have easily led to a lizard escaping, and/or you receiving a serious bite from a set of very sharp teeth. Besides it didn't look very professional. As if this was not bad enough I would always have the thought in the back of my mind that a past reptile keeper had had his calf muscle torn apart by one of the occupants, so they had had a taste of human flesh, so to speak, a thought that was always on my mind when entering the enclosure. Some days I had some very close calls and wonder to this day how I came through unscathed in all the times I fed them, without so much as a scratch. It got to the stage where I dreaded the task, leaving me feeling very apprehensive about the whole situation. On one very hot day with the lizards on full alert and eager to feed, I felt very apprehensive about entering the area. I was running behind time, I was tired, I had been working a very long shift, and the last thing I wanted was to attempt to go through the lizard gauntlet. The answer, however, was to throw the rats over the fence, and then enter the enclosure, which worked very well leaving me at peace to clean up after them. Although it was not the accepted practice, it was far safer, so I was happy when the enclosure was eventually decommissioned and pulled down many years later.

Underneath the Reptile House was another area that you had to bend down to enter, which we referred to as the dungeon, and for all intents and purposes it could very well have been used as one. It had several corridors that ran from the main area deep under the Reptile House. The main area accommodated several trays of meat-eating beetles, or dermestids as they are sometimes technically called. These beetles could strip the flesh off dead animals within weeks or months depending on the size of the carcass. Various departments would use the beetles to clean up carcasses for the education department or Melbourne Museum. Then once the beetles had done their job the skeletal remains could be glued together. Due to the rotting carcasses the area stank and at times was very difficult to enter, not being able to escape the smell as there was no ventilation. It was the place as you could well imagine we spent the least amount of time in.

On one side of the Reptile House were two lizard enclosures containing blue tongues and shingle backs or stumpy tails as they are sometimes called. It was well landscaped with rocks, plants and natural cover simulating their natural environment. On entering one of the enclosures to feed one day, I discovered that the surface of the enclosure in some areas began to cave in on me, and before long I was looking at a whole area of broken and smashed and caved-in polystyrene boxes. My work partner at the time had without my knowledge decided to bury some of these boxes to give the lizards some subterranean hiding areas. After informing him of the incident I believe he removed them with some degree of disappointment and disgust. So much for good communication, although it was a great idea at the time.

Feeding Frenzies

When feeding our snakes, whether they were on display or not, we would use plastic rubbish bins just for this purpose with lids that could be firmly secured. This would enable us to feed the snakes individually, as some snakes tend to be cannibalistic and also so we would know how many rats or mice each snake had consumed, as this was recorded on each snake's record card. Keeping in mind that each snake could be recognised by its unique markings or patterns.

We had four Forest Cobras on display, and they would at times be subjected to visitors banging on their window in the hope that they would rear up and display their hoods, which they almost never did. As they were very flighty they would do just that when we opened their enclosure to feed or clean. They also would strike and attempt to bite one another, so to use this bin feeding system proved to be very effective and safe. So it was not unusual on a feeding morning to see multiple bins sitting in the viewing gallery containing snakes consuming their food within them, prior to opening of course. Some larger pythons we would allow to venture out of their enclosures while we cleaned to explore the surrounds of the viewing gallery, we always kept an eye on them and would easily return them. One morning a visitor from another department was in the building with one of the Curators, she was totally shocked when she was confronted by one of the pythons. As we did most of our major feeding during the warm summer months it was always a busy and sometimes hectic time of the year.

Snake Handling

Whenever we had to move a snake for some reason or other we would use specifically designed snake hooks of varying sizes. If we had to restrain the snake for treatment we would use a square section of sponge attached to a rod that we could hold the head of the snake safely with, however venomous snakes presented a different situation as they could easily pull back their heads and bodies and have you rather than you having control of them, so it would take two keepers to conduct the restraint procedure: one to secure the head, the other to hold the body. Some techniques today have changed where venomous snakes can be moved into a clear solid plastic tubing, preventing them from pulling back or attempting to bite. Larger pythons, depending on their size, would involve multiple people to assist in restraining them.

A Bite to Remember

There would be times that one would get bitten. It's bound to happen at the best of times. One occasion I was bitten on the hand by a full-sized scrub python. It took several keepers to release it. No real harm was done, just a few puncture wounds and I was treated for my wound only to squeeze out several teeth from the wound site the following day.

Another major bite I received was delivered by a Western Massasauga Rattlesnake. These medium sized snakes come from Texas, Colorado and Mexico. They have a light-brown base colour with rows of dark brown blotches. One morning while working solo I observed that the female snake had given birth, to six young, as this species gives birth to live young rather than laying eggs. The male was positioned under a log near the front of the exhibit and undetected by me it struck out, resulting in a bite to my index finger. I then went through the process of picking up the snake bite emergency phone which put the call immediately to the hospital. I then with the aid of one of the zoo's cleaners who was in the building at the time, wrapped the bite area with a bandage and waited for the arrival of the ambulance. Via their radio television stations 9,2,7 and 10 received the news, and managed to arrive at the hospital before the ambulance. Upon settling into a room and the bandage removed, I waited in anticipation for any signs of envenomation with hospital staff beside me to gauge my reaction. While waiting, all the television crews burst into the cubicle to film and interview me, and barged through the privacy curtain, where I quickly requested them to remove themselves and leave me alone. After an overnight stay and being woken up every hour to see how I was progressing, I was back at work

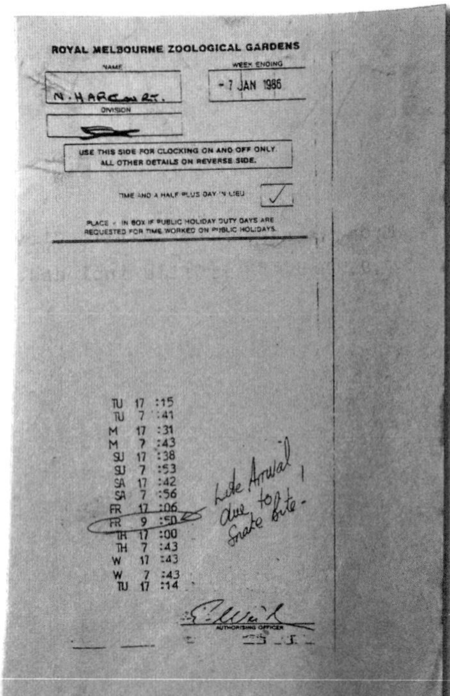
ROYAL MELBOURNE ZOOLOGICAL GARDENS

NAME: N. HARCOURT.

WEEK ENDING: - 7 JAN 1986

DIVISION

USE THIS SIDE FOR CLOCKING ON AND OFF ONLY.
ALL OTHER DETAILS ON REVERSE SIDE.

TIME AND A HALF PLUS DAY IN LIEU ✓

PLACE ✓ IN BOX IF PUBLIC HOLIDAY DUTY DAYS ARE REQUESTED FOR TIME WORKED ON PUBLIC HOLIDAYS.

TU 17 :15
TU 7 :41
M 17 :31
M 7 :43
SU 17 :38
SU 7 :53
SA 17 :42
SA 7 :56
FR 17 :06
FR 9 :50
TH 17 :00
TH 7 :43
W 17 :43
W 7 :43
TU 17 :14

Late Arrival due to Snake bite.

AUTHORISING OFFICER

the following morning, a little tired and late, but with good reason. Writing on my arrival card "LATE DUE TO SNAKE BITE". I'm sure that raised the eyebrows of the paymaster and gave me more than sufficient reason in being late.

There was always the odd occasion that you would be bitten by non-venomous snakes or a lizard that took exception to being moved or handled. One large gecko specimen from Asia almost took the top of my finger off one morning, a behaviour I had not expected, maybe word had got around. You just put it down as part of the process. That was my one and only venomous snake bite and I took all the measures in the Reptile House to keep it that way. I believe I am the only reptile keeper on record to have been bitten by a venomous snake, something that I'm not all that proud of.

Rattlesnake Roundup

While we are on the subject of rattlesnakes, I recall the day I arrived at the airport to pick up a Southern Pacific rattlesnake from the live cargo area. On producing the relevant permits and papers I was escorted into the main area which contained numerous boxes stacked against the wall and on the floor. It reminded me of the final scene in the movie *Raiders of the Lost Ark*, where the ark of the covenant is driven into a cavernous storage room with thousands of boxes stacked everywhere. When the staff who were sitting around having their morning break were asked if they had seen a box containing a rattlesnake I began to worry about the efficiency of this department. Surely they would have read the label on the box. Several workers got up and looked around, with one lifting his bulky frame from one box he was using as a seat only to ask, "is this it?" which indeed it was. As luck would have it the label did indicate that, and the snake was unharmed or should I say uncrushed. What followed was a series of phone calls from us enquiring as to why the rattlesnake was not held in a more secure area. We made the suggestion that there should be an area set aside for live animal imports or exports.

A Very Long Stint

As there were only two of us that could work the Reptile House round apart from the Curator who had other important issues to attend to, a situation arose where my work colleague was to go overseas to attend a number of conferences and to also look at other reptile facilities. This was to be for a six-week period and, as there was no alternative, I was to work without a day off for that period of time – unheard of in today's workplace practices. If I had taken the option not to work, my colleague would not have been able to go, he had been within the keeping fraternity for much longer than me and was well respected within the field. I felt obligated to cover for him. Prior to his trip I was able to take some time off to get my head around what was ahead of me and get myself in the right mindset. Daily procedures on any round are repetitious, and even though I had the support of the Curator it was a daunting thought to consider. However I felt that I could endure the process and that I would be in charge of the Reptile House, something that I could add to my achievements. I received no overtime rates or any increase in my wage other than to be paid for all the days that I had to work. As the days progressed I felt comfortable in the daily routine and took each day as it came, with regular correspondence from my work colleague.

The day did come that I came down with a bad case of the flu, and as I knew that there was no one else to cover for me I still attended, and at one time I had just barely had enough energy to perform the basics without putting any of the reptiles in the collection at any risk at all. I persevered through some three days and eventually was back to the normal Reptile House routine. Keepers from other departments would come down for morning or afternoon tea to see how I was progressing, as well as the Curator. At the end of it all I knew that I would never be put or put myself into another situation such as that. Maybe it could be looked upon as someone's nightmare to spend six weeks around a vast collection of reptiles.

A New Home for the File Snake

The only fully aquatic snake in the collection was an Arafuran File Snake, a largely nocturnal non-venomous snake, inhabiting lakes and rivers of Northern Australia and New Guinea. They do not have gills like fish but come to the surface to breathe. We were at the time having some fungal lesion issues with them that were proving difficult to treat. We housed them in a fish tank which was proving to be inadequate. After spending an unreasonable amount of time servicing the tank one afternoon, I gave considerable thought to facilitating the construction of a new aquarium to house it, not only larger in size but in a different location. There was an area directly opposite within the off-limit area that could accommodate such an aquarium. It would require cutting a significant square hole through the wall where it could be positioned. As I had previous experience with aquariums, I proposed the idea to the keeper in charge, who was immediately on board with the idea. I felt that through various avenues and contacts I could possibly get some or most of the equipment required for the project donated, with much of the work carried out by myself with the assistance of the maintenance department. Our budget was always tight, so cost to the department was a hefty consideration. After coming up with the initial design and dimensions, I was able to get the section of the wall cut away and a solid steel stand built behind it to support the 1,253-litre aquarium that had been specifically made for, and later donated to, the department. A large-capacity filtration system was incorporated into the aquarium. A fibreglass canopy was then made up to fit securely on the top of the aquarium, with service doors at the back. The aquarium was aquascaped with mangrove roots and vegetation, and the canopy was decorated with branches and tropical plants. Frogs were accommodated here and had access to the aquarium also. So the display not only housed file snakes, but Jardine River Rainbow Fish found in the same waters as the file snake, and Australian Green Tree Frogs in the canopy. This resulted in a naturalistic environment giving the viewing public a more stimulating file snake exhibit experience. I later wrote a paper on the exhibit for the International Zoo Yearbook, which was published by the Zoological Society of London, something today I still have a copy of, and remain very proud of.

We were always looking at natural furnishings to provide the reptiles with climbing space and to simulate a reptile's natural environment. The opportunity to secure some large, bowed branches from a bush property was quickly jumped on. This involved a day trip to the property to very carefully cut and remove the selected branches from trees and carefully winching them onto the back of a zoos tray truck.

After much effort and time we eventually arrived back late that afternoon with our load which we left secured, or so we thought, at the back off-limit area of the Reptile House, with plans to have them bolted into place in some displays the following day. Much to our surprise the following morning several of the branches had disappeared, only to discover after some investigating that the Manager of Works who lived on the premises at the time had come across them that night and chainsawed some for his fire, much to our anger and frustration. The untouched branches however were put to good use and made a great natural arboreal space for our pythons.

Snake Catching Encounters

The Department would receive a considerable number of calls during the summer months from members of the public who had a snake that had ventured onto their property. We would attempt to keep them reasonably calm and later produced a pamphlet called 'Snakes Around the House,' which we would post out to them, giving relevant information on the behaviour of snakes and the dos and don'ts when encountering them. Snakes are protected whether venomous or not, and to eliminate the possibility of a garden instrument being used to exterminate a snake, sometimes putting the user at risk of being bitten, some of us applied for and received snake-catching permits. This was a service that we provided outside zoo hours, and we would request a moderate catching fee that everyone could afford. The whole object to remove the snake safely and relocate it to an area away from human habitation. Later the local Council in my area paid me a service fee and employed me as the local snake catcher. Over many summers I captured snakes in swimming pools, laundries, wood piles and gardens. On one occasion I was asked if I would accompany some wildlife officers to a residence where it had been reported that the occupants had in their possession some unlicensed venomous snakes and wished me to positively identify them. I turned down the offer as I did not want to be involved in that specific area of snake catching, and I was not employed by them to carry out such a task. I was later informed that the said residence was at the headquarters of a local motorcycle club.

Some snake calls would come at an inappropriate time, such was the case one Christmas Day, just a few hours before sitting down to Christmas lunch with the family. I received a call from a distressed woman that a snake was in her backyard. After explaining to me the situation it became obvious that the intruder was a totally harmless blue tongued lizard, situated in a pipe in the backyard of her house. As the suburb she was located in was some considerable distance away, I attempted to inform the woman that no members of her family were at risk, and the unwelcome intruder would eventually move on, however she was not to be convinced and with a promise to pay me a considerable amount for my time, service and inconvenience I headed off to attend to the situation. An hour later I was sitting down to lunch with the family with a blue tongued lizard safely secured, with a wallet considerably fatter than it had been earlier that day.

The local Preston Leader newspaper published a full-page article titled 'Give Snakes a Break' about my services, which gave some great information regarding snakes. I also featured in another article in the Mail Express, a Melton local paper, after I had removed a large flighty tiger snake in the middle of summer, when it had made its way into the laundry of a Sunbury home. I charged just $65 for my services and removal of the snake, only to read in the article that the resident would have paid me $200 to remove it. I didn't mind at all if it was enough just to know that the snake was OK, going about its business in the bush, and that no one was bitten, or the intruder had not been attacked by one of the owner's dogs.

One of my colleagues who also provided the snake catching service visited a local gym on his way home from work, after he had received a call that a snake had been seen under a set of lockers. Sometime after arriving he safely removed a large red bellied black snake with a very moderate fee charged. Later that week the local paper from the area reported in an article that the zoo was charging people to remove snakes from properties, which was completely untrue. It was eventually brought to the attention of the zoo's PR department, and we found ourselves having to explain, which we felt we should not have had to do. We were angry that such an article had been released without any consultation with either the zoo or ourselves, and we contacted the paper and the journalist responsible asking for an apology, and to a statement in their paper retracting the misleading information. We received an apology but no follow up article. So much for false news.

On one other occasion several young boys presented themselves at the front gate on a hot summer's day with a full-sized Brown Snake they had caught in their backyard and placed in a shoe box. When asked what they used to catch it, they informed me that they just picked it up by the tail and placed it in the box. I'm still amazed to this day that they were not bitten, considering the speed and aggressive nature of this species of snake.

The World of Frogs

An area had been put aside for the sole representation of frogs. This space was once the sole classroom area for teachers to hold classes and attached to one side of the Reptile House. This room had been replaced by the Education

Classrooms, which was a major shift and improvement on school education in the zoo. As this area for the frogs was only small, it was an area that the department wanted to make the most of in representing endangered frog species. Previously I had made several contacts with staff at the Snobs Creek Fish Hatchery in Eildon where a close friend had utilised a fibreglass application that when mixed with natural materials such as peat moss and different grades of soil combined with mangrove roots and branches could create very effective natural backdrop environments for fish, this could easily be applied to frog exhibits. Snobs Creek Fish Hatchery was set up in the 1950s to produce salmon species for anglers. Although breeding initially focused on salmonids – that is Brown, Rainbow and Chinook salmon, the hatchery also began to investigate into the biology and reproduction of native fish species, to support conservation of threatened species. In the early 1980s native fish production began and now produces over 400,000 Murray Cod fingerlings for release into Victorian waterways.

Over time and several meetings my friend agreed not only to provide this revolutionary application within the World of Frogs, but to do it free of charge. This required him to travel to the zoo from Eildon on a daily basis and the incredible results can still be seen today within the World of Frogs, and I believe also at Snobs Creek Fish Hatchery. The frog complex is made up of eight frog environments housing endangered species of frogs such as the Baw Baw, Spotted, Eastern Dwarf, and Southern Bell Frogs. There is also an off-limit breeding facility which the public can have viewing access to get an idea of the dedicated work being done to maintain these amazing frogs, and the program that enables these species to be successfully bred and later released back into the wild.

Riding for Reptiles

It was a roster that I had with one of the keepers who worked on native mammals that we would carpool, as we didn't live all that far from one another. As the Reptile House on weekends didn't close till 5.30pm, my carpool buddy had a half hour to kill so he would ride his zoo bike down to the Reptile House, and as I closed the doors, checking all the locks as I always did before departing, he would ride his bike around the viewing area, sometimes gaining quite a bit of speed. By the time I was ready to go there would be a significant amount of bike tyre rubber residue on the floor, only to get a comment in the morning that there must have been lots of pushers in the Reptile House on the weekend, however I never disclosed the real reason why.

At that time all keepers would get around the zoo on departmental bikes, and we would often have a large plastic bag on our shoulders after a visit to the food store to collect fruit and veggies. It was a skill that we could pick up quite a speed as we headed back to our respective departments. One day I had reached a good speed on my bike while riding along a pathway, only to have another keeper coming in the opposite direction just missing me by millimetres. Some years later an education teacher had a nasty accident on one which put an end to the use of bikes in the zoo, much to our annoyance and disappointment. I recall that all the bikes were stacked up near one of the workshops and I don't know what their fate was, maybe they were released back into the wild.

The Drinks Are on Us

Directly outside the Reptile House were several drink dispensing machines. One hot day prior to the zoo gates opening one of the machines malfunctioned, resulting in cans being ejected one after the other. Upon filling the kitchen fridge, we reported the incident to the catering department, after all we felt that that was an adequate reward for reporting such an incident, hence we were well supplied with ice cold drinks, which saw us through the hot summer months that followed.

Cricket Plague

We maintained within the Reptile House live rats, mice, mealworms and crickets, all as food for the inhabitants. It took up a considerable amount of our working day cleaning and feeding them.

It was reported one morning that there was a huge cricket plague just up the road from the zoo. Even though I was the only one rostered on that day I was not going to let this opportunity of acquiring free reptile food pass by. So with several large fine nets and some large bins, I managed to spend some hours scooping up as many crickets as I was able. This resulted in a huge amount of free reptile food for the department and a considerable saving to the departmental budget.

CHAPTER 8

Let's Get Educated

After three years on reptiles I felt that I needed the opportunity to work with different species, and I applied and was successful in securing a keeping position within the Education Keeping Department which housed a huge variety of reptiles, fish, native mammals, birds, and a selection of small primates.

The Education area was built on site where the zoo's train once operated in the 1920s and grew over the years eventually covering a large circular rail line with grassed area in the centre and shelter sheds. A tunnel was used to lock up the locomotive when it was not in use.

The Education Keeping Department had some ten classrooms, where teachers could bring in pre-booked school groups. The rooms accommodated many exhibits including reptiles, birds, small primates, native mammals and fish, a huge improvement on the single classroom that was once connected to the side of the Reptile House. It employed some ten teaching staff and would accommodate up to 65,000 face-to-face experiences for students every year. It was one of the largest Zoo Education Facilities. The area also had a farm barnyard with goats, sheep, ducks and chickens, and this was used for children with special needs to have some hands-on experience with the animals. There were many education programs devised by the Education staff such as Pop the Pelican, Painters, Dancers, Poets, all were used as important parts of education units for all ages, also to give city living children the opportunity to come into contact with farm animals where they otherwise would not have.

The roster worked much the same as the Reptile Department, where you worked weekends solo. It was on one of my solo weekends when I left a trolley full of numerous food trays to be fed off to the huge collection. Where I left it proved to be a problem, and created much extra work for me that day, thanks to the resident goat that managed to consume almost the entire contents of the trolley, through the fence. To this day I've never been a fan of goats.

It was always a challenge to create natural environments within the classrooms, with large, secured branches leaning well out of the enclosures above the students, so they could look up during a lesson and see a Bearded Dragon basking above them, a great demonstration of natural behaviour. All the keeping staff had a free rein at coming up with ideas for natural environments for the vast range of species that we accommodated. One of the displays housed archer fish. These fish have a unique behaviour where they are able to shoot down various species of insects from branches above them, by a single jet stream of water from their mouths. We had created an open rainforest above their large aquarium, and the teachers could place insects above them so the fish would give a living example of their feeding behaviour.

Two of the South American squirrel monkeys that we had in one of the classrooms not only had a large indoor enclosure, but access to a large outdoor rainforest area, so they could retreat inside on cold or wet days. Squirrel Monkeys grow to only 25 to 36 centimetres, making them ideal for the illegal pet trade. They live in tropical forests of South America and live in large groups they are yellowish in appearance and have dark colouration on their heads around their eyes and mouth. They sweat through the palms of their hands and feet making those areas damp to touch. They lived for many years and enjoyed us being around and hand feeding them at various times. Students could accompany us into the enclosure to hand feed them and would often react to the Squirrel monkey's cold hands and feet.

Through the Education Section, secondary school students were able to apply for volunteering within the keeping department. The period of their stay was two weeks, and we would train them to a certain level giving them a taste of a zookeeping career. Their duties were mainly supervised and at times they were permitted to complete certain tasks without supervision. The good workers who showed a high level of interest and standards were of a great benefit. However there were always the ones who just looked at it as an escape from school and would stand around leaning on their rake or broom, showing little or no interest in their duties or surrounds. At one time a student disappeared for hours, only to find that she had taken herself off for a self-guided tour of the zoo grounds. These individuals proved time consuming for us to supervise, something that during a busy day we didn't have much or any time for, as they appeared to have little time for us.

After experiencing several weeks of disinterested students I was becoming frustrated and at one time instructed a student to go for a wander around the zoo as she was of no use to me. I put a proposal in place at one of our regular meetings, that if a student was not showing interest or did not comply with the work within the first week then they were to be sent back to their school. The new policy worked well, with students being told that this is what they would face if they did not meet our standards. The hard-working students would sometimes on their final day with us, bring in sweets or a homemade cake. Any staff member who was away or sick got little or no chance of getting a taste of any of it.

A Historic Discovery

One of the workers on the section was always into the historic aspect of the zoo. He had a vast collection of photos of old exhibits and would always take time out to photograph old exhibits prior to their demolition. While revamping the old train tunnel within the grounds of the department which we were using as a storeroom for fish tanks, possum boxes, tools and equipment, we decided to treat him with a discovery of sorts. We took some parchment paper and stained it with black tea and turned up the edges to give it the appearance of age. We then drew out lines of paddocks and displays as they would have been all those years ago, carefully making it appear legitimate. This took some time during lunch and tea breaks, and the end result astounded even us. Once rolled up several times with a tattered red ribbon around it, we tucked it away against some shelves and we waited with bated breath for the discovery. Once discovered by the intended person he was no doubt in awe of his find and showed us his historic find. The reaction was well above our expectations, and we had to somehow find a way of breaking the news to him that it was indeed fake. Once the word was out he took it on the chin and was appreciative of our effort, I believe he still has it in his possession today, maybe as a reminder of our skullduggery.

As we would often look at changing the classrooms into environments rather than just a room full of enclosures, we would always be on the lookout for large branches or rocks to be included into our environment plan. At one time one of the Education Keepers I was working with was installing a forest environment in one of the classrooms and had done a considerable amount of research on the preservation of pine needles. As my uncle at the time owned a property near Ballarat, we planned a visit with his permission to remove some large pine tree logs and branches to be incorporated within the room. Three of us headed off in one of the zoo's tray trucks and upon arriving we managed to get our fill of some great pine logs and branches. As it had been wet prior to our trip, and feeling rather overconfident, I managed to get the truck severely bogged and with the day getting on we were presented with the major task of getting ourselves out of the predicament. After placing all kinds of materials under the wheels and several hours later exhausted, we managed to free the truck and headed back. As there were other collecting trips planned after I was no doubt well aware why I was never invited to go again.

Magpie Magic

Magpies, while we are aware of their singing abilities, are also as we know or have experienced capable of aerial assaults. However there is more to them than meets the eye. They occupy the same territory their whole life and also become familiar with the people within that area. They mate for life, however if the male is killed while young are in the nest the female will take on a new male. When the young magpies are kicked out of the nest they are forced into poorer territories where they form gangs. They are also excellent mimics.

The Education Department got the opportunity to adopt a young magpie, and over time he would follow us around as we went about our daily duties. He would often sit on our food trolley or a nearby branch and warble away contentedly. He would also follow teachers and students into the classrooms, much to their delight, giving them a firsthand opportunity of getting up close to one of our most iconic birds. One morning while following a teacher into a room, who I believe was carrying mealworms, a magpie's favourite, he pecked at a teacher's shoe, possibly believing that she had dropped a mealworm. The teacher became concerned that he would have the tendency to repeat this pecking behaviour and possibly injure a student or keeper. In not wanting to take any chances he was donated to Ballarat Wildlife Park where he spent many happy years, until one fateful day he flew into the Tasmanian devil enclosure. I'm sure you can well imagine the outcome.

I have to this day several female magpies that come into the garden to be fed, they will even sit on my knee. However I don't feed them all the time as this can lead to them becoming aggressive. They are a delight to behold and are great company.

Hand Raising at Home

Animals were often brought into the zoo, and the pink sheet that the donor would have to fill out would usually have "Found, lost wandering in the bush" in the comment section! A tour bus driver delivered a small Olive Python in a calico bag to the zoo, he had come across it on the road and the tourists wanted him to kill it believing it to be a venomous Brown Snake. Olive Pythons are not venomous but are brown in colouration. Some possums would be looked after in the animal nursery, and we would be given the opportunity to take them home and hand raise them. I had a Ring-tailed Possum that I successfully raised and released. I called it 'Dead End' as it had part of its tail missing.

On one occasion I had to work on my daughter's birthday, I got permission to start work early on a Saturday so I could accommodate her birthday celebration within the Education Animal Area where my daughter and invited guests could have a party with a difference, amongst a variety of animals, and have the opportunity to come into supervised contact with snakes, lizards, wombats and kangaroos. My children would at times come into the zoo with me on my rostered weekends on and enjoy their time wandering around viewing the animals. They would often be invited to have some behind the scenes experiences in other departments, leaving them at times the envy of other children.

The Education Resource Centre was directly connected with the Animal Education Area and accommodated a large library and offices for the teachers who would take on lessons for booked school groups. It also was an area for other items that were stored such as wildlife videos. All staff members had full access to this building, which also could be booked out for conferences or other events. It was once the main kiosk and tearoom and was converted to the Education Centre in 1979.

I enjoyed my time on this department creating new displays and working with a huge range of animals. School students entered and left all the classrooms having a better appreciation of the animal world. Years later keepers made some major changes to the displays with one room being made up like a back garden with an old-fashioned toilet, unused of course, that housed frogs and spiders, larger snake enclosures were designed to look more natural and easier to access.

When a position became available on the Carnivore Department, it was offered to me, however with a catch. To cover staff going on long service leave the Marine Mammal Department, which was at the time a division of Carnivores, required someone to fill in. So to make my way to Carnivores it would have to be via this department. I had no desire to work with marine mammals and knew very little of them. But all that was about to change.

CHAPTER 9

Into the Seal Pool

The Seal Pool area was once a Monkey Island enclosure with a water moat some 7 metres wide. It was promoted by the zoo in 1938 as the Large Monkey Island and had no parallel in the Southern Hemisphere. It wasn't until 1942 that some monkeys managed to escape via a wooden trestle which was thrown into the moat by some mischievous boys. In 1953 it was converted into a seal pool and in 1971 the old enclosure was updated with mock rock formations. In 1987 'Seal Encounters' was developed, with the key feature being the installation of an underwater viewing window which was some 6 meters long and 1 meter high, giving visitors an uninterrupted view of seals swimming underwater.

The Keeper in Charge of the Marine Mammal Department was responsible for the complete transformation of the department and the seal husbandry, formulating a new water management system and training programme for working with the seals. It involved the introduction of some 12.5 tonnes of salt to the water with the salinity levels being maintained by introducing more salt to the pool to maintain the correct salinity level. Salt was added to the pool via a balance tank situated in the off-limit area. Some of the seals had experienced opacities in their eyes due to the water being unsalted, the introduction of salt water proved to be successful. A water testing regime was also established where the water was tested for salinity, alkalinity, hardness and chlorine levels every hour, and we could then make the necessary adjustments based on the results of these tests.

In its day the seal pool contained 484,000 litres of water. That's a lot of water to keep clean and clear. The water was filtered via a sand filter at rate of 60 litres of water per hour to filter all the water in the pool. It was not only the filtration plant that helped to achieve this but the also the daily vacuuming of the pool. To carry out this task one had to pull a cumbersome and heavy solid steel dark green cylinder so called portable filter system up several steps and along the public viewing pathway. Once primed – and believe me it took several attempts to achieve this – one would then proceed to manoeuvre the vacuum head, which was on the end of a very long aluminium pole, over the barrier fence and into the pool. Once this was achieved it was a matter of pushing the vacuum head back and forth along the bottom of the pool, tilting it slightly to one side when one encountered seal faeces. More often than not the system would stop sucking and one would have to go through the whole frustrating process of priming it again.

New arrivals to the department would always get the firsthand opportunity to experience such a pleasurable task, taking most of the morning to complete. Many years later one of the keepers wrote a paper on how to successfully remove seal faeces from the bottom of the pool without leaving any residue or skid marks – for want of a better word.

Other changes were made with increasing the variety of fish species we purchased. Slimy Mackerel, Yellow Tail, squid, pilchards, mullet, and numerous other species. The fish when delivered in bulk were kept in a large freezer, every day the amount of fish to be used for the following day was taken out and weighed and placed in a fridge to thaw out for feeding. Each seal had its own bucket and the amount of fish that each seal received depended on their age and weight. The fish purchased had to be of a high standard and anything less was rejected. If it wasn't fit for human consumption then it was deemed as unfit for the seals. The fish would be supplemented with salt, Thiamine, and Vitamin D tablets that had to be inserted into the fishes' gills when preparing them before placing them in the feed buckets. This all represented a huge increase in the department's budget, and seals had the highest budget of all animal divisions. In fact our male seal Lonely consumed some 5 tonnes of fish per year.

We had seven seals in the collection at that time; Lonely, Silva, Melba, Liz, Julia, Lucy and Calo. Five female Australian Fur Seals, one female Sub-Antarctic Fur Seal and one male Australian Fur Seal. Liz being the oldest, and Calo the youngest. Each seal had its own station that it would sit on at feeding sessions, and they were all expected to stay on their station unless we told them otherwise via learned hand signals. Each hand signal would indicate to each seal what they were required to do, such as jump into the water or present a flipper or vocalise, and of course they would receive a fish after each behaviour was carried out. It was all based on positive reinforcement, and any behaviour that was not asked for was ignored, and the seal would not receive a fish for such behaviour.

Only the Lonely

The Department had the largest and heaviest male fur seal recorded in captivity. Lonely was 400 kilos and was the very first seal successfully born at the zoo. During the breeding season he was isolated into a separate area, where he did not have contact with either the females or us, and we would feed him from the public side of the fence, explaining to the onlookers why we had him in this situation and that it was dangerous to go in with him or attempt to do any training sessions with him during the breeding season. Other times Lonely was a pleasure to work with and train. When swimming with the seals we would quickly vacate the pool if he began blowing bubbles through his nose which was an indication that he was not prepared to tolerate us any longer. During the public seal feeding sessions we would ask Lonely to exit the water and lumber up to us via a slope where we would put him through his paces and then get him to return to the pool. One particular afternoon after I had done a close-up session with him I gave him the hand signal to return to the water, which he flatly refused to do. Now this presented somewhat of a dilemma as my colleague had his back to me, training the other seals, so I had virtually nowhere to go. After several attempts to get him to move he eventually did, freeing us up to continue with our feeding of the other seals. A daunting experience in having such a huge male fur seal right in your face.

Moving the seals into their off-limit areas was always done in a positive manner, so when they emerged from the display they would position themselves on a plastic pallet to feed. Lonely would eagerly consume his fish whole as all seals do, and if one of them appeared to be not quite right he would cough it up leaving us with a face full of fish cologne. Even though the fish we offered the seals was always of top quality, it came down to some species of fish that they did not like.

Hi Ho Silva

One of our resident seals was Silva. She arrived at the zoo in 1988 when she was only eight months old. At the time she was dehydrated and had a deep wound around her neck, the result of plastic entanglement. It took some time to nurse her back to health and she remained within the collection. She was a great asset to the department, and she was used to put across to the public the message of the dangers of discarded plastic in the ocean, she was trained to retrieve plastic items from the pool. Silva knew all the behaviours; however she gained the reputation of being somewhat aggressive and at times impatient, which always presented us with challenges during feeding time. If for some reason we made her wait too long for her food she would begin to vocalise in an aggressive manner, and then she would begin to approach us. As we had not requested her to do this, we were not to reward her with food but to stand our ground and signal her to return to her station. In these circumstances it was rather stressful not knowing if she was going to attempt to bite us which would result in her feeding session coming to an end.

While feeding her in the off-limit area one evening she decided to leave her pallet station and attack the seal next to her, which resulted in a full-on seal fight upon which I calmly put the lid back on the fish buckets and used one of them as a seat, knowing that if I attempted to interfere in any way I would have been seriously bitten. They both eventually settled down and it took me sometime before they allowed me to vacate the area. It was always the standard practice that we would never attempt to exit an off-limit yard when a seal was next to us. We would wait patiently for the seal in question to lose interest and move away, eliminating any risk of being bitten.

Lovely Old Liz

The oldest seal in the collection was Liz, the mother of Lonely, Melba and Calo. She was the first seal that new keepers got to train, or be trained by, more likely. Liz was almost blind, so she had to rely on her whiskers to detect what was going on around her. Part of the training to get a seal to focus on us was to target the seal. This required us to make a fist and have the seal place its nose on it, that way we had its undivided attention. However being blind, and relying totally on her whiskers, we couldn't trust her to do this without the risk of being bitten, so we devised a target that was a stick with a ball on the end of it, and Liz was asked to place her nose on that. At times she would become impatient and tempted to snap at the ball assuming that it was food. All in all she did rather well considering her circumstances and lived a long full life within the department.

Julia

Julia came to the zoo from Portland after she took up residency in front of a supermarket. She was called Julia after Lady Julia Percy Island which is a seal colony off the coast of Portland.

Melba

Melba was the daughter of Liz and was named after Dame Nellie Melba. She had blunt teeth due to her habit of picking up stones.

Calo

Calo was the daughter of Cess and Liz hence the name CALO – Cess and Liz's offspring. Cess was long gone before I commenced on the department.

Close Calls

Along the outside perimeter of the pool were skimmer sumps that were accessed by the removal of a lid to clear and clean the skimmer baskets. On one occasion a lid was left open, only to have a school student disappear down it, fortunately without any injury. When the keeper in charge was investigating the incident he wanted to know who was the one responsible and upon further investigation he realised that he was the culprit.

On another occasion a senior staff member entered one of the balance tanks while the filter system was still operating, and had his rear end sucked onto an inlet pipe while he was under the water. If not for his determination and holding his nerve he would no doubt have drowned. The same keeper had his necklace caught under a ledge while swimming with the seals, which could have ended up tragically, but he managed to once again free himself.

Swimming Sessions

When all the major tasks were completed on the department it would be time for a swim session with the seals in our wetsuits, which had been donated to the department via sponsorship. We would venture into the pool much to the excitement of us and the occupants. This was a great stimulus for the seals and assisted us in maintaining a good relationship with them. We were always aware of how each seal was on the day and always kept our distance from Lonely the male seal. He wasn't at all interested in having any type of interaction in the pool with us. Sometimes during these sessions some seals would bump into us or buff us around, not deliberately, but that was the way they played at times and got a little carried away. One young seal came up from under the water at almost full speed hitting my chin, in the process splitting it open, and turning the water red with the incident looking like a scene from *Jaws*.

A seal bite was always taken very seriously. Seal mouths contain loads of bacteria that can turn a bite wound septic very easily, so it was always the process to pay a visit to the doctors to have it tended to. I have a scar on my arm that reminds me of some mistakes I've made that had resulted in a bite from one of the seals.

I was thankful for this as one day, due to my own fault, I was badly bitten by Melba and that could have resulted in a very serious deep wound. If ever a keeper received a bite or almost one we would as a department analyse the incident and discuss it to prevent it from happening again, we never blamed the seal in question, it was always an error on our part.

The Keeper In Charge and I, with our flashy wetsuits on, would not only swim and entertain the seals, but the visitors as well. Sometimes running out onto the seal display, jumping into the water with the unsuspecting seals, who would leap around us, delighted at having us in the pool with them. We would often run out of the display only to appear standing with the crowd. Much to everyone's delight we would strike up conversations with them, then jump back into the water.

We called ourselves 'The Flying Fandangoes' and always had great fun in putting on daily performances for the crowds.

Some seals would come straight at you when you were underwater, and then at the last minute, swim past you with millimetres to spare. If you happened to be in the scuba diving gear they would love to hover just above you, and mouth or remove just about every part of your gear much to the amusement of the seals and the public.

There were days that I would leave work absolutely exhausted from some lengthy swim session, most of which occurred on weekends, which we and the public enjoyed immensely.

The Keeper In Charge taught me a huge amount and I recall on my first weekend working with him, he got me to go out onto the public seal viewing area to observe him doing the usual weekend training session. There were seven seals in the display on the day, every one of them made their way to their stations. The session was amazing to see, where the results of his training program which he didn't have to brag about the proof was in the pudding. I will always have the greatest respect for him.

At times someone would come up with some other sideline activity that several of us would get involved with. One which the then Keeper In Charge and myself got into was breath holding competitions within the filtration balance tank which one could enter via a steel ladder attached to the inside wall. It was a large dark and deep area, and one would have to hold onto a step that was under the water to enable one to stay under the water while holding one's breath. The other keeper would stand above on dry land recording the time. Times recorded were posted on our notice board within the office and this activity became a regular competitive event. One I am sure would be frowned upon by management.

Wet Willies

One weekend late after a busy Saturday Session the Keeper In Charge and myself were getting changed out of our wetsuits after a long swimming session with the seals, it was already getting dark as it had been a twilight session and we both were ready to head home. However a package arrived, and on opening it we found what we had long been waiting for, our new underwater torches. With all the seals secured in their off-limit areas, and an empty pool calling us, we decided to venture back into it and put our new torches to the test. So minus our wetsuits, or any other form of swimwear, we entered the pool and oh what a delightful and free experience it was. That no one had ever done or thought of before it was a keeper first achievement for us and proved to be our last. Under the cover of dusk we tried out our new torches as we swam around underneath the water. Within a few minutes we both heard voices approaching the exhibit, it was definitely a group of people, and not visitors for they had departed long ago. We both stood directly up against the outer pool wall with torches off of course and waited. The group arrived looking into the seal pool directly above us, it was the Chief Executive Officer and some VIPs in tow. Remaining motionless we prayed that none of them would look directly down. Anxious minutes passed and they eventually moved on. I don't think that anyone has ever exited a pool as fast as we did. And if they had decided to look into the underwater viewing area I would hate to think of the outcome. A sight no doubt that would remain in their minds for years to come and ours as well.

From time to time the department would take on seals that were brought into the zoo, seals that had been found in coastal townships. Some when taken back to the seaside ended up back in the town in front of the local supermarket. Once at the zoo they were isolated within a suitable off-limit area where they were examined for any injury or medical condition. Some animals would come in with plastic around their necks or flippers, some were caught up in fishing lines or had swallowed fishhooks. Once they were treated, some would feed voluntarily, while others had to be force fed. Bear in mind restraining a seal is not an easy task and required several keepers to restrain the seal. One item of equipment that was used was a recycled solid plastic board, specifically built for the task, with sturdy straps attached so a seal could be secured on it and transported safely. Once a seal was feeding voluntarily and had significantly increased in weight, it was to be released and this involved a day trip down the coast to have the pleasure of being involved in its newfound freedom and of course have a swim with wild seals.

Seals that were assessed as not suitable for release were incorporated into the zoos collection. We never attempted to get any of the seals to balance balls on their nose, but for them to perform natural behaviours from swimming, showing how they groom with their flippers, and how they vocalise. This gave the public a perfect example of how seals are so well adapted to their marine environment.

We had a rehabilitation programme for seals that were rescued and brought into the zoo. Two such seals we named Coral and Cribbie. Coral was rescued from Queenscliff and was badly underweight suffering from mouth and stomach ulcers. Cribbie was recovered from Crib Point and was the smaller of the two seals. When found she was very underweight and had been tormented, receiving stabs from broken glass and lit cigarettes and offered hook baited pieces of fish. Seals such as these were housed in an off-limit area close to the vet hospital, tended to every day, and force fed to help them begin to feed by themselves and gain an optimum healthy weight. When fully recovered and feeding well we had a day trip to make to Popes Eye in Port Phillip Bay to release them. Diver Instruction Services, a long-time supporter of the programme, provided the boats for the release. Members of the media also attended to record the event. Both seals had been trained to move into large seal pet packs in which they were transported and loaded onto the boat. It was always extremely rewarding to watch the seals released back into the wild. We would dive into the water and basically find ourselves swimming with the wild seals and were always in awe of their speed and agility as they leaped over us.

Diving for Aquariums

In the underwater viewing area of seals an opportunity arose to install an aquarium, as a representation of the fish that share a seal's marine environment. The underwater seal viewing window was 52 mm thick and was installed in 1987. The front of the aquarium was made the same height as the seal viewing window to give it continuity. We had a contact with the Temperate Marine Fish Society, and arrangements were made for a visit to get some initial ideas as to what could be created. Upon seeing their plans, arrangements were put in place for one of us to join them to collect some species that we could accommodate in our newly installed up and running aquarium. I was selected to go diving off the Mornington Peninsula with them. We took the boat equipped to provide divers with oxygen lines, and I got my very first experience of diving. While swimming around watching fish being netted, I had the feeling that something was watching me. As I turned around I came face to face with a seal, a wild one this time, which swam around me and then took off into the depths. Not to forget to mention that the incident was almost followed by an explosion from my rear end. The aquarium was set up and proved to be a very successful enhancement of the underwater viewing area, representing a good variety of temperate marine fish species.

Otoliths and Lake Mungo

While working on the Marine Mammal Department and while on holidays in Mildura with the family, we took a trip to Lake Mungo which is a dry lake located in NSW. We received a full guided tour of the area, visiting several old fire sites along the way, which gave the group the opportunity to look at various animal bones within them. At the last stop we sat around the remains of a fire, upon which our tour guide proudly produced a small oval bone and passed it around the group, me being at the very end, hence the last person to view the item in question. It took me one look to know instantly what it was, an Otolith, the ear bone from a fish. I looked up across to the guide and noted the look of 'no one will know' on her face, which got me to ask myself the question will I or won't I assist her keeping her secret. The guide's face went ashen when I correctly identified the object, and it appeared to have all the blood drained from it, later while walking back to the car park the guide with the now white face came running up to me to ask how in hell did I know what it was? I informed her that while working seals and vacuuming the pool on a daily basis I would encounter hundreds of them passed in the faeces of the seals. She informed me that to date no one had been able to identify the item, I often wonder if she ever regretted taking out the item on that day.

I enjoyed the years that followed on the department and learnt a great deal about seals, something I never would have experienced otherwise.

The American Connection

The Director of Melbourne Zoo put together a program to allow zoo staff to travel overseas to gain firsthand information from other institutions, and to get ideas that could be applied back at the zoo. In 1992 I was given the opportunity to travel overseas to the USA to look at aquariums, due to my passion for fishkeeping and my desire to see further representation of more fish species within the zoo. My itinerary was North America taking in New York, Baltimore, Chicago, Seattle, San Francisco, Vancouver and Honolulu aquariums. I chose these aquariums for a reason: New York Aquarium being the oldest continually operating aquarium in America, Baltimore that had been built during a period of urban renewal and runs as one of the country's leading aquariums, Chicago's Shedd Aquarium is the third largest aquarium in the Western Hemisphere, Vancouver Aquarium with its tropical gallery, Seattle Aquarium with its huge 1,500-litre aquarium, San Francisco's Steinhart Aquarium which is one of the most biologically diverse aquariums, and last but not least on my visiting list Waikiki Aquarium in Honolulu, the second oldest aquarium and the first institution to breed Nautilus Molluscs which are related to squids and cuttlefish.

Travelling for some three weeks there were highlights aplenty with incredible environments and systems with plenty of huge freshwater aquariums representing fish from all over the world. I had the opportunity of seeing large South American species of fish that I had only read about, as well as major environments incorporating mixed species, which was a great stimulus for one's sight, sound and smell. Rainforest environments housing freshwater stingrays, sloths, squirrel monkeys, all in the one tropical area with intermittent rainstorms and simulated cloud shadows moving above you.

New York Aquarium is situated in Brooklyn and in 1992 was an area that you had to take care when walking around in. After a day of being escorted around the facility and even taken out for lunch by one of the curators, I said my farewell, only to be told that he would drive me to the taxi stand just down the road. It didn't take long for me to understand why as the area itself was not what you would call all that safe. I was even watched by the curator as I walked to the centre of a major road and asked for a cab from a large individual who was the taxi controller. He waved to a cab a considerable distance away and soon I was sitting in the back seat on the way back to my Manhattan hotel.

All continued to run well with my schedule until I arrived in Vancouver. I had previously stayed in hotels or with keepers, however I had failed to secure a place to stay in Vancouver and upon arrival at the airport was informed of a lack of accommodation due to a conference that was going on in the city. After some searching and assistance from staff at the airport, I was directed to Gas Town, a local tourist area where I could possibly find a place to stay. I eventually did in what was a very basic hotel with only one room available, which I paid for three nights in advance. Feeling rather fortunate that I had found a place to stay during my visit I made my way to my room. However after a quick inspection I discovered cigarette burns on the bedside table and the window giving me a full view of a brick wall. Well, it was better that nothing, I supposed. Being late in the afternoon I ventured out into the streets to acquire a meal, which I found at a small side street restaurant. After ordering and waiting for my meal I witnessed one individual being chased down the street after robbing a store, and several drunks who were laying around as well as a drug dealer who wanted to offer me some of his wares. I later ventured into the downstairs bar of the hotel only to find all eyes on me and not all that friendly ones. After a restless night's sleep with loud music vibrating up from the bar I made several phone calls and managed to find that a vacancy had become available at one of the top hotels which I eagerly took. Upon registering at my new accommodation the receptionist asked me where I was going and where I had been, in mentioning my Gas Town experiences he informed me that no one who valued their safety should stay overnight in Gas Town.

The remainder of the trip was uneventful, and I was grateful to have had the opportunity of visiting some of North America, I came back with some great memories and concepts that could be applied to Melbourne Zoo. One being to implement more fish species within the zoos collection.

Fish are today represented within certain areas of the zoo.

CHAPTER 10

On to the Meat Eaters

After my time on Marine Mammals and having covered for staff to take their long service leave, I eventually was transferred onto the carnivore department which at the time had a large collection consisting of big and small cats, bears, badgers, otters, Red Pandas, and Meerkats, just to name a few.

The keeping rounds varied depending on the carnivores that were within them, and new keepers to the department were trained, as with all departments, to a very high standard, with extra emphasis on safety due to the dangerous nature of some of the animals.

Big Cats and Small Cats

It's not just a matter of size but a whole lot of other factors that separate the two groups of cats. Big cats can roar due to the elasticity of the hyoid bone in their throat, which is connected to their mouth and tongue. Small cats have a rigid hyoid bone, so they are unable to roar. Big cats have round pupils, where small cats have elongated slits. As per their size, big cats have larger brains, but domestic cats have the ability to learn and develop behaviours due to their closer relationship with us. Both are hunters and sleep for long periods of the day, sometimes up to 20 to 22 hours.

However there are some exceptions to the rule re the big cat/small cat equation. The Puma and the Cheetah are the odd ones out, as big cats are included in the genus *Panthera*, small cats are under the genus of *Felis*. Pumas also fall under this genus. Cheetahs however are under a separate genus of *Acinonyx*. So why are they different even though they are much larger than small cats? Well, it's that pumas don't roar, and they communicate via a series of squeaks, growls, hisses and even screams, and other tonal sounds. Cheetahs can chirp, purr, growl much the same as pumas. Cheetahs do not have retractable claws which aid them to have a good traction when running at full speed. They hunt by day, and they easily give up prey if challenged. They also have great elasticity in their back when running at full speed. They have a relatively small head, small ears, and eyes that are set high. Rapid acceleration requires a high degree of oxygen intake, so they have enlarged nostrils to take in maximum amounts of air when at full speed. So size isn't everything in the cat world.

Some Facts About Cats

The only cats that we have in our lives are domestic ones, unless you work with them as I did in a zoo.

Some years ago my daughter, who works in the domestic animal field, was assisting the vet with an unfortunate case of a small litter of kittens that had been brought into the clinic. Their mother had passed away and they were all in terrible condition. As the decision had been made to euthanise them, she was assisting the vet and noticed one of the kittens crawling over her siblings, vocalising loudly. She made the call to take it home and hand raise it. As it had not been weaned the kitten had to be fed every two hours and also treated for lice and other issues. As time progressed the kitten made great progress thanks to my daughter's passion and commitment. We eventually fostered her and then adopted her as part of the family. Tilly now is just over two years old and it's great to have a cat around the house.

Domestic cats as we know them are very popular as pets but there are a number of obligations that we have as cat owners. We are obliged to provide them with an appropriate living environment, access to good health care, freedom from fear and the opportunity to act out their natural behaviour. We also need to provide them with a good diet of dry and wet food. When it comes to milk, it's important to note that cats are lactose intolerant and giving them cow's milk can actually cause significant health issues, such as stomach upsets and other related issues. Lactose-free milk has a high amount of sweeteners and calories and can also have a negative effect on your cat's health and wellbeing. The domestic cat as we know it has a number of traits. They are intelligent, due to a high level of brain power. They have excellent hearing; they can move their ears independently of one another. They have an excellent sense of smell, and they rely on this to identify certain deposits that other cats might leave around. They also have excellent night vision taking in their nocturnal surroundings. They also have a great ability to make full use of the family home having access to more areas than we do. Cats purr when they are contented by sitting on our laps or licking us. This is a form of communication and also ends up as reciprocal situation of keeping one another warm. They possess an armoury of scent glands on their bodies from the face to the feet down their tails. It's important just like exotic cats that they are provided with enrichment items and cat towers as they like to get up in to elevated areas. One of the most important issues is that we should be aware of the capabilities of cats when outside. They will prey on native birds and mammals as hunting comes naturally to them. A great alternative is to give them access to an outside enclosure and keep them inside overnight. Cats sleep for many hours during the day, and upon waking spend time grooming themselves. There are numerous facts that you can find out about your domestic cat, and to find out more about them gives you a better understanding and relationship with them. Melbourne Zoo currently has an area set aside that covers this subject and is useful information on responsible cat ownership. It's always interesting to get to know more about your cat.

Maya and Me

Maya was a huge black or melanistic male Jaguar. Jaguars are the only living big cat native to the Americas. They can reach a length of some 1.8 meters and weigh as much as 160 kg. They are excellent swimmers and are one of the most endangered species.

An incident occurred when I had cleaned Maya's enclosure, and in the process of giving him access I felt that he had moved into the outside area rather differently. I was to attend a meeting and on the way up I felt that something was not quite right. As I was to clean his off-limit area on my return I felt that I needed go back and check right there and then. On looking into his night den I observed that he had in fact doubled back on me and was waiting near the den service door for my return. I knew that I would have checked anyway but it would have just taken a split second for me to overlook this and open the door. Instinct had prevailed much to my relief and Maya's disappointment.

Another hide and seek game that Maya would play is when we released all the big cats out onto display we would walk along the public viewing area observing each cat to see that they were eating ok and behaving as they should. Many times, not seeing Maya, you would learn on hot days to look in his pool to see him submerged with just his eyes and nose looking directly at you, hoping that you would venture into his realm looking for him.

We had made available to us some bulls heads that a farmer had delivered. This, for carnivores, is the best form of enrichment, and we were always on the lookout for opportunities to provide them with such items. We placed one in Maya's off-limit area, and when he came in that afternoon he went straight to it licking it and chewing at the flesh and bones. He then decided to take it into his den, but due to the horns he was unable to do so, so he was just as contented to eat it outside. On arriving in the morning Maya had somehow managed to get it not only into his den but was sitting with it up on the bench. Most or all of the flesh had been eaten away, and he had made considerable impact on the bones of the skull. When it was time to let him out on display he once again attempted to go out with it in his mouth but after several unsuccessful attempts he took it back onto the bench and remained with it for most of the day. The only solution we had was to place a sign out on his display informing the visitors that the jaguar would not be out on that day. By that evening there was not much left except the horns and a few remnants of the skull, it was indeed a great event for him.

Another piece of enrichment that we put in his off-limit area was a very old tractor tyre. He relished it and pushed it around and sat in it and even dragged it from one side of the off-limit area to the other. We even placed some meat in it, and it didn't take long for him to pull it out and consume it. By the following morning he once again amazed us, as he had dragged the tyre halfway into one of the off-limit den's doorway. It took us a considerable amount of time and manpower to remove it, and we subsequently hung it from one of the steel beams so he could no longer use it as a door block. These were actions by Maya that gave us a reminder and appreciation of his sheer strength and determination, and the reality of how dangerous and powerful he was.

Maya and Muana

We had been pushing for another jaguar to accompany Maya in the collection, and after some consultation a surplus female was found and had become available from a European zoo. I was the fortunate one to go out to the airport to pick her up (or could have been not so fortunate). Upon arrival at the cargo area I was directed to a smallish box parked on a pallet off to the side of the cargo building. Even from a distance it looked rather narrow to contain a full-grown Jaguar. It was painted green with no bolts or padlocks only some long screw bolts holding the end shute doors down. It wasn't all that solid either being made of plywood which concerned me even more. Picturing a jaguar on the loose at the airport was something I wasn't prepared to even imagine. Upon lifting the end flap of hessian I was confronted with a snarling jaguar peering at me through a window only covered by chicken wire. She had no water, and I asked one of the cargo workers if he could get me a container of water. The jaguar drank at least a litre that I had poured into the rusted tin container, and then my main objective was to get her on the truck and back to the zoo as quickly as possible.

My colleagues were just as amazed as I had been when I arrived back. Upon getting her to the facility where she was to be housed we placed the box in her new off-limit area and fastened a chain onto the top of one of the box shute doors. This would allow her to go straight into a den as this could be carried out safely from above. On attempting to lift the door it was obviously jammed, so we had to turn it around and lift the other end door which we managed to do. Once secure in the den we noticed that her front paws had been bleeding, and she was rather dirty due to the narrowness of the box. Apart from that she appeared ok, which the vet confirmed. Upon removal of the box the reason for her blood-stained paws was revealed, she had in fact not been able to turn around and had subsequently ripped up part of the floor in sheer frustration or stress. If it was not for the metal underlay she most certainly would have escaped. So much for the movie *Snakes on a Plane*. We also found out that she had been in the box for longer than she needed to be, due to the lack of paperwork from the zoo she was transported from. After a few phone calls we discovered that she had been delayed for some time at a major airport due to insufficient paperwork, and there was no other alternative provided other than her spending an unacceptable amount of time in her shipment box.

It took her several weeks to settle into her spacious enclosure and it took her some time to venture onto grass or wood chips, which indicated to us that she had been previously housed in a very small concrete enclosure. She was introduced to the male Maya but unfortunately they never reproduced. They did however live many good years together. I loved the name Muana, after all it was a name I bestowed upon her.

Hutan and Me

One of our resident Sumatran tigers was Hutan, one of three tigers born at Melbourne Zoo. Tigers are endangered, there were nine subspecies of tigers, three of which are now extinct, being the Javanese, Balinese and Caspian. Leaving only six subspecies remaining; being the Bengal, Amur, South China, Sumatran, Indo-Chinese and the Malayan tiger.

Hutan shared the exhibit with his sister, and we would alternate them during the day giving them time both on and off display. Hutan was a somewhat nervy animal and would get rather annoyed if something unexpected occurred, like most animals, but his reactions were most always over the top. Windy days at the zoo were always a reason for concern, any large branch from one of the many trees on the property could come down across fences or into exhibits, so we would either secure animals in off-limit areas or give them access. One particular day a huge storm came over the zoo, resulting in several trees coming down across the property, with one large tree falling near the back of the tigers' exhibit. Fortunately, it did no damage falling across one of the off-limit pathways. The theory goes that as I was the next keeper Hutan saw after the incident; he assumed that I was the one responsible for such a thunderous act. His attitude towards me became one of complete and utter fear, possibly thinking that I was capable of tearing down the odd tree now and again when the urge to do so came upon me. He would pace and keep as far away from me as possible, anytime I was within the immediate area, he refused to move past me or come off display for me. This was great reason for concern as you don't decide if you can work with some cats, they make that decision for you. After this consistent behaviour I came off the round not wanting to stress Hutan out any longer, and any relationship that I had with him ceased, much to my disappointment and despair. To lose the trust from an animal as a keeper is devastating.

Animal training plays a significant role in zoos and has great benefits for animals and keepers alike. One of the keepers had received a scholarship to attend training workshops and programs overseas, and she was well versed in all areas of training and behaviour. We got together to discuss the issues that Hutan had with me, and she observed firsthand his aggressive and fearful reactions towards me. She was as surprised as I was with his behaviour and set up a program with me to set things right. At first it was me just being at a distance from him and staying low to reduce my appearance as being too obvious. His reaction never changed, as soon as he saw or heard me it was enough to set him off on a stressful rampage. After some time spent reviewing the situation a plan was put in place, that was that if ever Hutan was to be fed it was I who orchestrated it, coming in, placing the food down, and then leaving. This we carried out as much as possible, even with me placing food through the wire of the off-limit area. The plan had to be consistent with no changes, as animals can be stressed from this. Weeks passed and it got to the stage that the behaviour was never going to change, but winners never quit, and quitters never win so we persisted. However the day arrived that I came in solo to feed Hutan, expecting him to run to the opposite side. Instead he walked towards me slowly but surely before moving away without any fear, and after several days he eventually took the meat that I offered him through the wire. I had to control my utter relief and disbelief, as you could well imagine. Hutan over the following weeks continued to accept me again and eventually our relationship was restored, and I could once again work with him. Many years later after I had left the zoo, while leaving the zoo after attending a function I walked past the tiger enclosure to see Hutan laying down. As it was late in the day and no one being around except for the group that I was with, I called out his name, he immediately lifted his head and looked directly at me, holding his gaze. I knew without any doubt that he recognised me, and it was an exceptional moment, I not only felt a huge amount of satisfaction but honoured that he had recognised me after so many years.

Adventures in the Lion Park

African lions have always maintained their popularity in zoos and have been given the title of King of the Beasts. They are the only big cats to live in prides. A lion pride may consist of up to three males and many females with young. All the lionesses and cubs are related. At around three years of age young male lions leave the pride and will possibly move on to challenge other males for the control of a pride. Males will protect and defend the prides territory while the females take down prey together to feed the pride.

The zoo's old Lion Park, that has since been replaced, was built in 1967 and was a watershed for the zoo, as it not only housed some nine lions but seven African wild dogs in an adjoining enclosure. The public could get an uninterrupted view of it all via a bridge over the middle of the two. The oldest lion that we had within the pride was Spring, the matriarch of the pride. Early one morning it was observed that Spring had passed away and was laying in full view at one end of the park. As the opening hour was not yet upon us it was all hands-on deck for the carnivore crew. We were able to get all the lions into their off-limit dens apart from Jespha, Spring's daughter, who chose to stay close to her deceased mother. After several unsuccessful attempts to get her to move into a secure area we were presented with a serious dilemma. After reviewing and discussing the situation there was only one option, that we would drive the van into the lion park and attempt to get between Spring and Jespha and drag Spring's lifeless body into the van via the van's rear door. Jespha was indeed stressed, as were we in this situation, but we had a limited amount of time to rectify this, and it was our only option. Staff were positioned at either pathways to the park to keep away other members of staff who were not aware of the situation. I was the designated firearm person. As luck would have it, upon opening the main park gates and driving in, Jespha moved a considerable distance away which gave us the time and space to haul Spring's lifeless body into the van. It was such a relief that I didn't have to find myself shooting Jespha, resulting in two deceased lions, but just aiming the rifle at her went against all my principles as a keeper. The postmortem that followed showed that Spring had died of natural causes due to her age. Lions can live like most animals in zoos far longer than they would in the wild. Jespha gave birth some years later to six lion cubs, the biggest litter of cubs recorded at the zoo, consisting of five males and one female. We used a roster system allowing several cubs to feed at a time from their mother due to Jespha having just four nipples.

Lion Brothers

There were two male lions, Kruger and Tsavo, in our pride, brothers that the zoo had acquired from New South Wales. Both got on quite well and over time it was observed that when the two had an altercation, which brothers often do from time to time, that Tsavo always appeared to come off second best and over time had collected some nasty facial scaring. Tsavo had been the dominant male, but it was obvious that his position was being compromised and Kruger was now the head of the pride. We decided to anaesthetise Tsavo to check some of his facial wounds, and to give him a once over health check. Moving and managing a large big cat for such a procedure requires planning, such as isolating the lion and not feeding him prior to the visit to the vets. Staff are allocated certain tasks on the day such as assisting the vets or moving the lion onto a stretcher. A designated firearm person was always present in case of an emergency. Once anaesthetised Tsavo was checked via a rod to see if there was any eye or ear movement, indicating the depth and impact of the anaesthetic. Once cleared he was lifted onto a stretcher and driven to the vets. Upon investigation it was soon discovered that he had had his front claws removed prior to coming to the zoo. So now we knew why he was coming off second-best against his brother.

'Holden' On

To promote a new Holden model of car the zoo was approached by the car company about a public relations exercise to demonstrate how solid this new model was by placing it into the lion park and allowing the lions to have their way with it. For our involvement the zoo would be given a new Holden van that the Carnivore Department could make good use of. We felt that this as well would be a good enrichment program for the lions, but we wanted to make sure that they would not injure themselves or present any danger to them and that the whole process would be observed, over the days that the vehicle would be in with them. To make it more interesting for the lions we decided to smear the windows and the bonnet of the car with blood to make it more appealing to them. It took the pride some time to venture close enough to the strange intruder to investigate. It didn't take them long to prove that the lion is mightier that the car, even the two males managed to pull it several times. Then it all began to fall apart as sections of the car and wheel guards were violently removed, and holes appeared in the lower areas of the body work, windscreen wipers became separated from the windscreen, and after several days the car was taken out once the lions had lost interest, sending the designers back to the drawing board. The story got worldwide exposure through all the major media networks. The department in the end got the new vehicle that we made good use of for many years, and in the end it was a good public relations exercise.

Heads Up

It had been a busy day on the department with several keepers away on leave or ill. The last chore of the day was to feed the lions and as we were pressed for time, we decided to give them a horse's head that we had recently received some as a donation. The lions relished our offering, dragging the heads around in the long grass and settling down to a good feed, which would keep them occupied for days. As it was late in the day there were very few visitors around, but we were on hand to talk and explain the food items on that day to any concerned visitor. One gentleman approached us and had his suspicions confirmed that the food items were indeed horse heads, and then calmly reminded us of fact that the that the following day was Melbourne Cup Day. So much for timing.

Strop and Shelley

The Carnivore Department had within its big cat collection two Black Leopards, one of the nine subspecies of leopards. They are endangered and vary in size and markings depending on the subspecies. They are the smallest of the big cats but are the most adaptable. Strop and Shelley were Melanistic or Black Leopards. Strop would often come up to the wire fence of the off-limit race and place his paw just underneath it, he would then wait in the hope that you would get close enough for him to put his whole front leg through in an attempt to claw you, but we never fell for that one. If we needed to get onto the wire roof of any of the cat displays we would always secure the cats in the off-limit areas first as they were capable of leaping to great heights onto the underside of the roof and attempt to claw you through the wire. Strop was a master at this and to observe him leaping up from a standing position was indeed inspiring. Sometime after the female Shelley passed away from old age, Strop was observed lying in his off-limit area unable to move his hind legs, it was obvious that he had developed a problem with his spine. Darting him from the safety of the off-limit fence had no effect on him and he still remained alert even after several attempts. It was obvious that the injury to his spine was not allowing the drug to take full effect, and it was decided to venture in with him and restrain him. This involved someone with a firearm and someone to secure his head against the ground with a large broom, I accepted the task of manning the broom while one of my colleagues had the firearm. To walk into the same area as a snarling and growling leopard was very daunting, and the thought went through my mind as we entered his domain that this was a trick that he had decided to pull on us. We managed to restrain him with a cargo net placed over him for added security. The vet staff then eventually were able to get him to the vet department where it was found that the issue with his back was real and permanent and age related and he was subsequently euthanised, a sad day indeed.

Just Puma Luck and On the road

The big cat round consisted of six enclosures with off-limit yards that we could run cats into when servicing their enclosures. In between each enclosure was a keeping service area which gave us access to the enclosures, night dens and off-limit yards. A wire covered corridor ran the full length at the rear of the complex. We housed up to six species of cats which meant up to some sixteen animals at any one time. Today it exists no more, demolished to make way for new exhibits, however the dens remain and were incorporated into the new complex.

Pumas, also called Mountain Lions or Cougars are native to the Americas. Their range spans from the Yukon, British Columbia, the Rocky Mountains and areas of the western United States. They are usually solitary by nature and are crepuscular, that is active in the early hours of the morning and at dusk. We had a pair of resident pumas at the time. Our ageing male Puma had been ill for some time and after a vet examination it was found that he was in an advanced stage of cancer. However it was determined by the vets that his quality of life was good, and that he was comfortable and pain free under medication. He shared his enclosure with a female where he spent what time he had with her. Eventually he passed away peacefully. Some 91 days later the female gave birth to three young, two males and one female. We calculated that he must have somehow had the strength to mate with her days before he passed away. She gave birth one night unexpectedly, as no mating had been observed, and she had shown no signs of pregnancy. We were however delighted that the male had left such an amazing legacy. At eight weeks of age the young kittens, as they are called, were due for their first set of vaccinations. This involved securing the female into the night quarters and netting the kittens. We had a new keeper who had joined the department recently, and to give him firsthand experience we allocated him the female to catch and restrain as we believed that she would be the easiest of the three. However she proved to be the feistiest, but the new keeper was up for the challenge and handled the situation extremely well. Several years later two of the cubs were transferred to Canberra National Zoo and Aquarium to take up residence in a newly revamped and designed enclosure. The National Zoo and Aquarium was opened in 1990 and consisted of 30 different species and a large restaurant and function area with its main feature being a 1.5 million-litre aquarium with an underwater viewing tunnel. Later that year the aquarium was placed on the market and went into receivership in March 1991. In 1998 after some turbulent times it was purchased by the Tindale family. Over the years they repaired and replaced many areas of the facility. This included the discovery that the 1.5 million litre aquarium's concrete walls were showing severe weaknesses resulting in the system being deemed unsafe to hold that significant amount of water. The area was then modified to house the Pumas, and they could be viewed through the existing glass panels.

The operations manager and I were given the responsibility of transporting the pumas by road in heavy duty transport boxes firmly secured onto the back of a tray truck. The trip started in the very early hours of the morning when there would be less traffic on the road, and we could easily make the 600 odd kilometre journey in a day. We would stop from time to time to check on the pumas and to have a quick break. It was at one of the truck stop stations where we were asked by a burly and well-muscled truck driver what we had in the back of the truck. We informed him that they were Mountain Lions, another name for Pumas, he laughed at what he thought was a joke only to stop in his tracks when he realised that that's what we were transporting. One of us would always stay in the truck when we made a stop to prevent any curious onlookers getting too close.

Upon arrival it took some time to coax them out from their transport boxes, but once out they quickly settled in and explored their new spacious home. We stayed for several days and had the opportunity to look over the zoo and its expansive collection. Sometime later I was flown up to complete some accreditation on their Carnivore facilities and safety working procedures which I found to be state of the art. The zoo has continued to grow over the years and is very impressive to say the least.

Small Cats

There are some 33 species of small cats in existence today, many of them endangered or vulnerable due to habitat destruction and being hunted for their skins.

We housed eight species of small cats within our collection ranging from bobcats and lynx to servals and ocelots, some names you may not be familiar with. Most of our small cats we could go in with but at times at our own risk depending on the cat. The caracal's colouration varies from various shades of beige to tawny brown, they have long black-tufted ears. In fact the words 'karra kulak' in Turkish mean 'black ears'. It is a medium sized cat native to Africa, the middle East, Pakistan and India. One of our caracals was aptly called Crack. Now Crack had glowing green eyes and he took great pleasure in not being visible when we entered his display, but once everything was raked and cleaned up he would appear at the gate making ominous growling noises and glaring at you with his iridescent green eyes, daring us to attempt to get past him. We would always have a rake with us of course, and that was how we distracted him. We just simply held out the rake in the opposite direction to the gate, and Crack would be on it showing no mercy, while we exited unscathed pulling the rake away from him as we went through the gate. When it came to feeding time speed was of the essence as most of the cats would be at or near the gate. During one feeding session Crack lunged from the open gate onto the wheelbarrow containing rabbits that were to be fed off. The quick-witted keeper quickly picked up the rabbit that Crack had attached himself to and threw them both back into the display. Amazing reflexes.

Crack shared his abode with two older females, Niala and Laini, one being partially blind and the other almost deaf. They were both otherwise in good health, however the deafness and eye issues would at times cause a conflict between the two as they would attempt to come into the off-limit area via the same shute door, resulting in a scuffle, with neither being aware of the other.

Two other residents were a pair of ocelots, Ripley and Trish, a beautifully marked small cat from South America, the Caribbean Islands of Trinidad and Margarita. They have beautiful distinct spots that put them in a very vulnerable situation re poaching for the pet trade, or for their skins. Trish the female was very approachable whereas Ripley was not. Ripley had a permanent limp due to past surgery on his right front leg. While Trish at times would rub herself against you, Ripley would always be looking for an opportunity to attack you and would constantly growl in distaste at your presence. If I was on the round just the sound of my voice was enough to set him off and I would always be on guard checking his night box if he was still in it. One fellow keeper was a victim of Ripley's aggression. While bending over Ripley lunged onto his neck. It was the one thing we felt he was incapable of doing due to his leg. I believe that Ripley felt that he had finally achieved his pinnacle after that incident. The keeper who was subjected to the unexpected attack came out of it with a few scratches and marks on the back of his neck.

Vaccinating the small cats was then a major operation taking up the majority of the day with several keepers and a member of the Vet Department. The practice then was to venture into the displays, net each cat, and hold them down wearing gloves of course while the vet administered the injection, and then release the cat without injury to the cat, vet or keeper. I have vivid memories of the day that I was attempting to net one of the cats in the off-limit area, only to miss and have the cat bounce off the head of my work colleague, without injury I might add.

Our resident lynx would lounge on a branch above us as we entered the display and would attempt to remove any head gear we happened to be wearing.

One of the first things that we would do during the round was to inspect the top of the enclosures to remove any possums that had been injured or killed as they made their way over the top of the enclosures during their nocturnal travels. The current possum population within the zoo is no longer at risk as the last of the small cats passed away many years ago. I'm sure the possum population is thankful for that.

One species of small cats that the zoo maintained and bred was the Asiatic Golden Cat, listed as a very vulnerable species. Golden Cats are from India, China and Southeast Asia, and are one of the most stunning of exotic small cats with reddish to buff brown coats, and their numbers are dwindling due to deforestation and being killed in revenge for preying on poultry. The department successfully bred some fifteen Golden Cats, a great achievement. Golden Cats are very secretive and will make every effort to hide in their night box or somewhere they feel safe. In order to help them overcome this fear and become used to us being around the area so we could observe them better, a fully dressed window shop dummy was placed just outside the off-limit areas in the hope that this would do the trick, I would like to think that it worked to some extent.

Golden Cats are one of the oldest inhabitants of the zoo, having been there for fully sixteen years longer than Mollie, the zoo's famous Orangutan.

One other small cat we had great success in breeding was the Asiatic Fishing Cat, a medium sized cat from South and Southeast Asia. Their front toes are partially webbed, and their claws protrude slightly even when retracted. They are excellent swimmers and fish catchers. We would provide them with fish, mice and day-old chickens. We had a large plastic pond that they would often get into. This was a situation that we wanted to improve, and we decided to construct a much larger natural-looking concrete pond for them to fully submerge themselves in. We had to relocate the cats and remove the front wire of the enclosure to give us full access.

We not only had to dig a significant hole in diameter and depth but had to wire steel rods together to give the pond strength before mixing and applying the coloured concrete, carving lines and curves in it before it dried to give it a more natural appearance. It was summer and the work was slow and hot, taking much longer than expected. However the day finally came when we could proudly look at our finished pond. The fishing cats once moved back took to the water in their new pond with relish.

Several weeks after the pond was installed a Natural History film crew wanted to obtain footage of fishing cats doing just that, fishing. They installed a glass panel in the wire to film through. Most of the filming was done at night as fishing cats are nocturnal by nature. Over several weeks they obtained some excellent footage of fishing cat behaviour.

Makulu and Twiga

Everyone is familiar with giraffes, and although they are herbivores they were at the time incorporated within the carnivore department. Makulu our resident male giraffe passed away at the zoo aged 23 years. One of the most iconic photos was taken in 1995, when he was just days old, with his mother Misha kissing him on the head. As well as appearing on the front page of The Western Australian newspaper the photo can also be found on the walls of countless living rooms, including mine. He was the first Rothschild Giraffe born in Australia for some 55 years.

He died due to weight loss and worn-down teeth due to his advanced age. During his time at the zoo he fathered four calves. He was approximately 5.5 meters in height and weighed around 1.25 tonnes. He was what you would call a gentle giant and was instrumental in delighting many visitors who came to feed him behind the scenes. Twiga the female arrived in 1997 from Perth Zoo. The only thing to separate us from the giraffes when we did our daily feeding presentation was a line of large rocks that they would not attempt to step over. Makulu would stand by you and accept his favourite food, being cut up carrots and some tree branches. We would be able to get him to stick out his tongue to show the visitors how long it was some 45.5 cm. He was an absolute gem to work with and he would move into his shute every morning to have his hooves checked while he was fed carrots from the front. The handling shute was installed and all the giraffes were trained to enter it safely, from the outside the padded panels could be swung open to give staff safe clear access at certain levels. The shute was initially used to treat Makulu for a skin condition, and slings were installed to hold him upright while he was given sedatives during the treatment process. Giraffes have a long way to fall when they are anaesthetised, so shute and slings kept him safe and upright during the treatments. The skin biopsics showed that Makulu was allergic to lucerne and acacia. A further series of drugs was administered to control his allergies successfully. The news of his passing was hard to take, even though I had left the zoo at the time, I had made it a firm habit to visit him from time to time.

Making Wishes Come True

One organisation that we had close links with was Make-A-Wish-Australia, a charity enabling children who were under treatment for various life-threatening diseases to have an opportunity to have their wishes come true. When it came down to a meet and greet with their favourite animal, we were always willing to assist and made every effort to make their experience a very special one. On one occasion a young girl who was obsessed with giraffes was escorted down to the giraffe off-limit area where I took her in to meet and hand feed Makulu. We had been made aware of her terminal condition and prior to meeting her I purchased a toy giraffe from the gift shop and presented it to her. She squealed with delight and with some encouragement she was able to feed Makulu and spent a considerable length of time with him.

Several weeks later I received the sad news that she had passed away. I have to this day a photo taken by her father of me with her holding the toy giraffe, in front of Makulu. It was something that made me more aware of my fortunate career and meant so much to me that I was able to put a smile on her face that day.

While visiting the Royal Children's Hospital to feed the resident Meerkats I observed a young boy who was aided in walking with some leg supports moving very slowly towards a recycle bin to place his empty plastic drink container in it. I observed his determination, and his parents were encouraging him all the way and clapped when he managed to stagger back to them. It was all too much for me and with teary eyes I sat down nearby in awe of what I had just witnessed. With the hospital shop nearby I raced in to purchase a soft toy and will not only remember the look on his face but his parents as I presented the well-earned gift to him as a reward for such an accomplishment.

Moving a Tall Order

So what do giraffes have to do with carnivores, you may well ask? Well, at that time the 'Savanna Round' as we called it was part of carnivores, it not only included giraffes but zebras as well. Every morning after checking our rounds every Carnivore Keeper would meet at the Giraffe Paddock to rake up the huge amounts of giraffe faeces, that the giraffes had deposited overnight. This would take a considerable amount of time but was always good for keeper bonding and giving time to sort out our day, as we endlessly raked amongst the dust storm that was created. One of our resident male giraffes, Jandamarra, was destined for Werribee's Open Range Zoo, so plans had to be put into place for pre-shipment. Now most animals like a routine and if that changes there needs to be a plan in place and strict communication between staff involved to achieve the best outcome for all involved. A large open shipment box was placed just outside the off-limit back gate of the giraffe enclosure. The giraffes, observing that it was something new, would walk over to look and touch it with the noses. Over time they accepted it as part of the norm and at times would take no notice of it. Once it got to this stage we moved the box into the enclosure, once again creating curious reactions. When this was accepted as well, we opened the side of the crate which would allow the giraffes access to it and offered them food within it, creating a positive place for them to enter into. It was only a matter of time before the giraffe who was to be moved would walk freely up and into it as part of the normal daily process and would comfortably feed within it. It was at this stage we would look at shutting the door and different stages with the giraffe in it until we could close the door and leave the giraffe in it while feeding. Once we were all satisfied with this stage, plans could be made for the moving date. A truck would come on site to lift the box containing the giraffe onto the back trailer and the move could begin. Plans included beginning very early one Sunday morning when we knew less traffic would be around, even the power and tram lines en route at a major intersection had to be lifted via a local council crane so the crate and giraffe could safely fit underneath. The going was slow with the giraffe enjoying the experience. It was amusing to observe the faces on the people that we passed as we made our way to our destination wandering no doubt that what they were seeing was real. The whole journey and move went without any problems apart from the giraffe wanting to feed from the trees along the side of the road.

The Meerkats at Myer

If there is one animal that everyone is familiar with it's the Meerkat, so many images abound of them standing upright on their hind legs. Meerkats are small mammals connected to the mongoose family and are found in South Africa. They have broad heads, long snouts, largish eyes and thin tapered tails. They live in large family clans or gangs, and work together with one or two Meerkats placing themselves on guard duty looking out for predators while the others search for food. The alpha pair typically reserve the right to breed and produce offspring. They will fight ferociously with members of other clans to protect their territory, which can be extensive in size.

The six Myer windows in Melbourne's Bourke Street Mall were installed in 1956, the brainchild of a Fred Asmussen, who was the head of displays at Myer. It was a gift to the City of Melbourne. Every Christmas the windows would display a festive theme much to the delight of the onlookers. The idea of a Meerkat display in the windows came at the right time when we were in the planning stages of installing a full glass front windows to the front of their enclosure at the zoo, to allow the public an unrestricted view of the thirteen residential Meerkats as they went about their day. At one stage the Myer windows had accommodated several men who lived in a makeshift kitchen, bedroom and living rooms on full display so the passing pubic could talk to them via an intercom system. This proved to be very popular, so Myer were on the lookout for something different to accommodate their windows. Myer had come up with the idea of some sort of animal and due to their appeal and popularity Meerkats were earmarked.

We met with the Myer team to see how we could make all this happen, and also to give the Meerkats a great form of enrichment and total change of environment it would also solve the problem of us having to relocate them elsewhere in the zoo during the installation of the new windows.

The Myer team were ready to provide us with whatever was needed without cost being a factor as every expense would be covered by them, and after several meetings the project went into full swing. I was elected as co-ordinator of the project, many meetings followed as to off-limit areas, safety airlocks, the size of the area at the windows etc which all met and exceeded our recommendations. And no, just in case you're wondering, we were not going to use them in a Christmas display as this was the winter of 1997. Myer made it clear that they had no intention of using the display to promote any products which they sold.

A large wall of plywood with a diorama painted on it was installed at the back of the area with a keeper access door. As the windows at the time were 41 years old and had been acquired at great expense to Myer, we had large Perspex sheets installed on the inside of the windows to prevent scratching from the Meerkats. After several weeks of construction and with the display completed several tonnes of sand was delivered and Myer staff who were more than eager to be involved, not only took delivery of the sand but also moved it into the display after hours which was a major task in itself. Everything was accommodated for including a keeper off-limit area equipped with a fully stocked fridge, and a taxi service set up to drive us to and from the zoo.

It now was all set and ready for the inhabitants. We moved all the Meerkats in the early hours of the morning and kept the window blinds down for several days to give them time to settle into their new temporary home. The idea was to use the speaker system to conduct several Meerkat feeding presentations every day, as well as the usual task of cleaning and making sure all Meerkats were ok. So as the electric blinds would rise, we would be ready to do our Meerkat talk. All in all it operated extremely well for all concerned, with me and another keeper working a roster system. On one occasion during one of my talks the Meerkats suddenly scattered into their night dens as a result of two large dogs on a leads looking in on them, it was no doubt the first time that they had encountered such a sight.

At the end of the two-week period at Myer the Meerkats were safely returned to their new revamped enclosure at the zoo, with all thirteen Meerkats having seen a glimpse of city life on the other side of the wall.

Meerkats and Magpies

A group of Meerkats were transferred from the zoo to a large glass fronted exhibit at the Royal Children's Hospital. Being a permanent display it was included on the Meerkat Round, and a bike provided to assist the keeper on the round to cycle to the hospital three times a day, to maintain the display and feed the Meerkats. This proved very popular with the children and their parents as they waited on treatment. I was allocated onto the round for some seven days which gave me the opportunity to do some major upgrade work on the display furnishings. One of the main food items offered to the Meerkats were live mealworms, and on returning to the zoo via the parkways I would inevitably come across several magpies and would offer them some of the left over mealworms which they would eagerly consume. As the week progressed I ended up with quite a few magpies following me as I rode my bike, some even flying just above my head. By weeks end I had a total of some 30 hungry eager magpies escorting me to and from the hospital. On my next day off the unsuspecting keeper, whom I failed to inform of my magpie feeding program, was inevitably mobbed by the magpies. So much for my Pied Piper days.

A Fatal Error

A day that I will always recall, as much as I don't want to, was a baby Meerkat catch up day to have them vet checked and to receive their first set of vaccinations. As we had some thirteen plus Meerkats running all over the place it was rather hectic. The idea was to catch the youngsters, weigh them and have the vets check each one out, then release them. It was done in the display prior to opening hours. Meerkats are fast and even at a young age can deliver a nasty bite. As a young Meerkat was running towards me I knelt down to capture it and at the same time as my knee met the ground the Meerkat went under my knee and was instantly crushed. I was devastated as this was exactly the opposite to what zoo keeping is all about. I had caused the untimely death of an animal and a young one at that. I got support from my colleagues, and it took me some time to get over it. A tough lesson to learn and whenever catching up Meerkats with younger keepers, I would always make them aware of what could happen.

During the same process many years later a keeper to whom I told this story to and reminding my colleague that anything could happen when dealing with a large group of Meerkats accidentally left a Meerkat in a holding box overnight when it should have been returned to its enclosure. No fatality occurred but a lesson learnt and passed on. Experience is a brutal teacher when it comes to working with animals but a very good one, that made us all aware of what can happen at any time.

Bearing it All

We had three Syrian Brown Bears – Honey, Sorrel, and Roan – all related. Syrian Brown Bears are native to the Middle East and the Caucasus Mountain range where Asia and Europe meet. It is the only known bear to have white claws. They can weigh up to 250 kilos, although they are considered to be a relatively small subspecies they are, like all bears, extremely dangerous. As the males Sorrel and Roan reached maturity they began to be less tolerant of one another, it was deemed time for them to be separated but not before they had one last go at one another. This was serious and both bears took a hold of one another while standing on their hind legs. Sorrel grabbing Roan's bottom lip while Roan kept a firm hold on Sorrel's ear, roaring and savagely shaking and pulling at one another. When they both got tired they stopped and took a breather while still standing upright and maintaining their hold on one another. Then, once rested, they continued their fight for several more minutes. We eventually managed to separate them by discharging a fire extinguisher in their general direction. They did not cause any damage to one another, but it was a sight to behold. One wondered what incredible damage they could inflict upon us.

Surprisingly the female bear gave birth. Even though she had been on contraceptives, but for some reason she still fell pregnant, giving birth to three cubs, one female and two males. This birth presented a dilemma as to the number of males within the exhibit and the existing space that the existing enclosure could provide for them. There was also the additional problem that the adult males could no longer be housed with one another. So in order to make it all work we had to arrange a roster system allowing the mother and cubs out on display for several hours, then allow the males to go on display one at a time. As bears have a long life span it left us with a very difficult situation as we did not want to cause boredom and stress with the bears so every effort was made to accommodate them with keeping staff spending more time with them and providing them with numerous enrichment items on and off display. As male bears are difficult to manage as they get older and that other institutions preferring females to males, we wondered how long we could maintain them in such a situation. At one stage the subject of euthanasia was considered, it was decided by the then Chief Executive Officer of the zoo to continue to maintain them, as there was no other area within the zoo that could accommodate them. Eventually luck was on our side and a zoo in New South Wales took on the two young males which was a major relief and a great outcome for all concerned.

Pandamonium Part 1

Giant Pandas were first documented by a Frenchman, Perl David in 1869, and in 1936 the first Panda was held at Brookfield Zoo in Chicago. In 1963 the first Panda was born in captivity at Beijing Zoo in China. In 1978 the first giant Panda was bred as a result of artificial insemination, at the time there were only seven zoos that housed giant Pandas outside China. Their numbers in the wild at that time stood at about 700 to 1000. Pandas are fully protected in China. Pandas are cyclical in behaviour, eating bamboo and sleeping. They may spend some 12 to16 hours a day eating bamboo which is high in fibre but low in nutrients, so they have to consume large quantities of it every day.

In 1988 two giant Pandas named Xiao Xiao, a male aged four, and Fei Fei a two-year-old female, came to the zoo from China for a three-month visit. The male was found wandering in the village of Xiao, hence its name, and the female was found as a starving youngster, presumably abandoned by her mother. The giant Pandas were escorted from the airport by fifteen security guards, several police and Zoo Staff. This was the result of some four years of negotiation between Chinese and Australian Governments. It was the first time the Pandas had left the Baishuijiang Nature Reserve. As a new Gorilla Rainforest Exhibit was being constructed at the time, the zoo was able to accommodate the Pandas in a section of that new exhibit, before the resident Gorilla group was transferred into it.

An observation room was available for VIPs. Huge lines of people could be seen outside the zoo grounds waiting to see the Pandas, at one stage nearly sixteen thousand people flocked to the zoo in one day. Many people were employed part time to accommodate the extra demand and duties from ticket taking, crowd control and serving in the two temporary large marquee Panda shops that had been set up just outside the exit to the display. Sales far exceeded expectations, and the shops had to be restocked sometimes several times during the day.

A person was employed to oversee merchandise and to make sure that all shelves were fully stocked. It turned out that he achieved far more than his job description, being caught out early one morning while taking a delivery back to his home, where he had previously on many occasions had come into the zoo during closing hours to make his special deliveries of Panda merchandise to his residence. This resulted in him being immediately dismissed and handed over to the police where his huge giant Panda stash was discovered and removed.

Some 656,000 people queued to see the Pandas and the highest attendance in one day, was 15,959 which assisted the Zoo in reaching some 1.5 million visitors for that year. I believe that Panda merchandise reached the $1,000,000 dollar mark. We had a celebration event at the end of their visit presenting certificates or awards to the hard-working people who put in long hours to make it all happen.

Pandamonium Part 2

The Red Panda, also known as the Lesser Panda, is much smaller than the Giant Panda and is red and white in colouration, native to the Himalayas and Southeast China. They are not related to the Giant Panda but are closely related to raccoons, skunks and weasels. Early one morning one of our Red Pandas managed to escape the confines of its enclosure by jumping onto the fence via a night box that was close to the perimeter fence. It took several hours to locate him in the Parkville parklands outside the zoo and after some misguided information as to its whereabouts he was finally netted and returned to his rightful place within the zoo grounds, with the offending night box moved of course.

Another Red Panda many years later made its escape and was detected on the top of the Lion Park fence. After securing the lions and wild dogs into their off-limit areas we went about devising a plan to net the escapee. However due to an impatient staff member attempting to single handedly capture the Panda it took refuge high up in the nearest tree. A cherry picker being used in the zoo grounds at the time was borrowed to successfully remove the Panda from its lofty loft. Even then it made another run for it only to be swiftly netted and returned to its enclosure.

Who Let the Dogs Out?

In my early days within the department I was servicing an off-limit facility which contained several African Wild Dogs. I opened the shute door to isolate them from the yard, and ventured in. As I was raking up the area I had a feeling that I was being watched, and on turning around both dogs were standing directly behind me. I managed to bolt to the gate and in the process of letting myself out one of the dogs managed to get through it as well. So here I was watching the wild dog run up to the off-limit area gate and come running back towards me. I yelled out to the keeper who was in the office adjacent to me, but my yells at first fell on deaf ears as he thought that someone from the adjoining golf course on the other side of the zoo's fence was cursing himself for making a wayward shot. He eventually realised my situation and came running up with a large hoop net and with one swift well directed movement had the escapee well restrained and contained. At the briefing that soon followed which was the standard procedure when such an incident had occurred, I was questioned as to what happened and without any hesitation took the sole blame, that's all they wanted to hear and the situation for me was a massive learning curve. Later it was discovered that a loose bolt had prevented the shute door from fully closing, nevertheless I should have checked the door and maybe would have discovered the loose bolt.

Wild Dog Roundup

At one stage we had seven African Wild Dogs which occupied a section of the Lion Park with the alpha pair giving birth to a substantial litter. In almost the centre of their area was a large cave or burrow that the wild dogs could retreat to. When the pups were around two months old and due for their first vet check and vaccinations, we were able to separate the adults into their off-limit yard so we could venture into the burrow to retrieve the pups. This was easier said than done, as one had to crawl with the aid of a torch into a dark and terribly dusty space. There I was confronted, yes I was the lucky one, by the pups eager to defend their space creating more dust to dominate what air space there was. In removing them one by one from the confined space and at the end of it all I looked like a human dust ball and smelt like a million Wild Dogs. Even though they are called Wild Dogs they are technically speaking related to wolves and have a caring social structure. Wild Dogs have a large range of vocalisations from short alarm barks to squeals, chirps and twittering totally unlike a dog. They are obligated cooperative breeders, usually only a single pair within the pack will breed. Pups that are old enough to eat meat are given preference at kill. They also look after older or sick members of the pack, bringing back food from a hunt and regurgitating it for them. Being social carnivores they are able to exploit a wider prey spectrum and can bring down larger prey as a group. We would feed them whole carcasses that would give a perfect example of their feeding behaviour.

Binturong Bust Out

They are called 'Bear Cats' in their native range of southeast Asia. They are carnivores but don't just eat meat deriving protein from small chicks, rats, and mice, along with a variety of vegetables as well as hard boiled eggs. They are rather lethargic in their movements and are nocturnal by nature. They are the largest of the civets and have scent glands for scent marking and after working with them for long periods, you end up smelling something like popcorn. We had a pair of Binturongs that resided in a circular enclosure which they shared with several Asian Small-clawed Otters. Binturongs being arboreal would spend a considerable amount of their time in the trees, however they would come down from time to time only to be attacked by the angry otters that would snap and jump towards them. The Binturongs would rise up on their hind legs to lessen exposure to their underside, and quickly retreat to the safety of the trees. This presented issues at feeding time and feed trays placed on the ground were later put on platforms in the trees, to enable the Binturongs to feed in peace. Years later a new enclosure was built to accommodate the two species, but we were not keen to have them in together. As well as issues with the close proximity to some bushes and trees that could provide the binturongs with escape routes, they would once again have to share the enclosure with the obnoxious otters.

The otters were moved first then the Binturongs. It only took a few days for Juna the male Binturong to make good his escape and he was eventually discovered one morning curled very high up in one of the nearby trees. It didn't make catching easy at all and after some pruning of the tree he was placed back into his new home. It appeared that the issue had been overcome until a week later he was discovered once again in another tree. As he was now wise to us he began to move around keeping his distance from the unfortunate keeper who was sent up to catch him, but after several hours we managed to net him and then moved him and his partner to one of empty small cat enclosures that was available at the time. We gave them both adequate arboreal spaces and later they were moved to a revamped enclosure where they could live in peace without the noisy aggressive otters and no chance of escaping.

Years later they were moved to a large, remodelled bird enclosure that was so much more suitable for them. I still have the pungent memories of their unique musky odour and easy disposition.

Aged Care for Carnivores

One section of off-limit yards ran down the side of the zoo wall within the department and was utilised to house older resident carnivores. One being

Strider, a Coati closely related to raccoons and like its cousins the size of a large house cat. It has a ringed tail and lives in trees and on the ground in bands of up some 25 individuals. The Coati is widespread occupying habitats ranging from Southwestern USA to Arizona, New Mexico and Uruguay. Females will only tolerate sexually mature males during the breeding session and after several weeks of vigorous matings the totally sexually satisfied male is chased away, sometimes resulting in him being injured. As Strider had been introduced to our females over the years he had fathered numerous young, however he had lost an eye from an altercation with one of the females but had maintained a great breeding record. Other residents were two Fennec Foxes which are the smallest species of foxes and most notable by their ears which can grow to 15 cm. They reside in the wild in North Africa, throughout the Sahara Desert where they inhabit sandy deserts with grasses and scrub vegetation. One female was called Farrah, after the actress Farrah Fawcett. One other Fennec Fox lived to the ripe age of 13 when they only live to some six years of age in the wild and only nine in captivity, an impressive record. The area no longer exists but those of us who worked the facility enjoyed making the aged carnivores comfortable in their later years.

Looking after older animals requires that they receive special attention, as some were in palliative care, and it was important that we would observe them on a regular basis and give any medication required. Cats that have a chronic condition may develop weight loss, not drinking adequate amounts of water, and just stopping eating all together. We would sometimes weigh them or spend time watching them eating as this would give us an indication of any problems with their teeth. Some being in an advanced stage of palliative care would be housed in the vet department.

The Slaughterhouse or CDPC

The Slaughterhouse at the zoo is the oldest in the Southern Hemisphere and we renamed it the CDPC, The Carnivore Dietary Preparation Complex, preferable to the word 'slaughterhouse' if wanting to mention the building on the two-way radio in earshot of visitors.

The Carnivore Department at that time had a collection that required some 4 kilos of fish and yabbies, 125 rats, mice and day-old chickens, ten goats, rabbits and sheep to feed all the carnivores in the collection in a single day. So you could imagine the expense generated over a year.

The department had a specific supplier of live goats that would be delivered in the early hours of the morning, usually when I first arrived, and then herded into the back of the Slaughterhouse for processing later on. We didn't like to keep them there for too long and would agree on the day we would slaughter. This was not what we always wanted to do as part of our duties, but it was a necessity at the time, feeding a large collection of meat eaters is very expensive and we were always on the lookout for any suppliers. We were trained to carry out the unpleasant task and we would arrange a roster, so everyone trained got the chance to collect the 'Slaughterhouse Allowance', not that it was much but a keeper's wage was not huge so every dollar counted. Once a goat was bolt gunned, a very humane way of dispatching with livestock, it was taken into the Slaughterhouse, winched up, gutted and skinned. Its carcass was then hung in the freezer and the remains binned and disposed of. With two or three of us carrying out this task and some 15 or 20 goats to process it was arduous and very tiring with the aspect of cleaning up after and cleaning out the Slaughterhouse sump – a task no one liked doing. It was not only goats but sheep as well. We would sometimes go to livestock auctions or travel to farms to pick up unwanted stock. Most times we would take delivery of dead goats or sheep which made it much easier on us in not having to do our own slaughtering.

I can recall one day when a huge black goat was in with the group of goats out back in the holding yard due to meet its maker. Some staff members were standing off to the side, one with the bolt gun which was used to discharge a hole into the sheep or goat's skull. They were apprehensive as to approaching the goat which I could well and truly understand it as it was bowing its head and showing aggressive behaviour. Being in not all that good a mood, I snatched the bolt gun from the colleague's hand, marched into the yard, grabbed the said goat and dispatched it in one easy movement. Then marching out of the area placing the gun back into the keeper's hand. I felt some anger relief at the expense of one large black aggressive goat. Maybe I had thoughts of that food stealing goat on the Education Department all those years before.

One year when Victoria was experiencing a bad drought, the availability of goats and sheep was at a premium, and we found ourselves going to sheep sales at the local yards bidding against more experienced bidders from major supermarkets. We would come back with a few which was always better that none. My father had a friend in the country near Ballarat who was running several thousand head of sheep, which due to the drought were not in peak condition, so we arranged to pay a slightly higher market price for them. He had on his property a slaughterhouse where he would slaughter his own sheep to supply his butcher shop. We even slaughtered the sheep for him at no cost, so it was a win-win situation for both parties.

Some months later we acquired some goats once again from another friend of my father, to help him out. It was tough times, and we were always ready to go way beyond to have what we once took for granted. Some years later we were offered free of charge sheep, fully dressed and hung ready for export to the Middle East, that had been rejected due to some freezing temperature issues. Pallets of prime meat were delivered to the CDPC and some of it found its way onto our dinner plates at home, due to the copious amount that we had. This once again saved us from the timely and unpleasant task of slaughtering.

When feeding in the Carnivores Department we adopted a policy that involved whole dead carcasses fed to the wild dogs, lions and small cats. This would generate examples of natural feeding behaviours but eventually raised issues with some visitors. This unfortunately led to changes in feeding that included the carcasses being cut up prior to feeding.

Run Rabbits Run

There was such a time that we would take delivery of many pairs of rabbits as they were always used to feed our small cat collection and also other carnivores. One staff member had informed us that rabbits were close to plague proportions near where she had a holiday property, so after consulting with the Senior Animal Manager we were given permission to arrange an overnight shooting trip to the area. Two other keepers, who were capable firearm personnel, and I, were selected to go. Upon arrival at the area and having the appropriate permission we soon discovered that there was indeed a plethora of rabbits. With guns in hand we ventured out in different directions, and it did not take long for us to bring quite a haul back to the car. After several hours we had more than our quota and made our way the nearest hotel for a meal. We got to know the publican over the time we were there and after we made our way back to the bush where we set up our camp for the night, we once again ventured out for some night spotlight shooting. Late on that night as we were settling down to get some sleep, we were awakened by someone calling out my name which was rather disconcerting to say the least. As it turned out it was the publican checking our story out. We returned the following morning rather tired but very satisfied that the trip had turned out well above our and the zoo's expectations.

Firearm Response Training

I inherited my grandfather's shotgun, so I learnt how to use it at a young age and got rather skilled at it, later on purchasing a rifle. I would go rabbit shooting quite often on one of my father's friend's country property, sometimes selling rabbits at the local butcher shop. Most zoos rely on firearm-trained staff to be on call in the case of an animal escape. Some overseas zoos rely on the local police force to deal with such issues, something I've never agreed with, not because they are not capable, but they have no experience in animal behaviour. An escapee could easily be shot for no reason. An animal could be hunched in a corner baring all its teeth in sheer fright, not willing to move, and be fatally shot by the police when it could be darted by a vet and anaesthetised to live another day. I remain today as one of the longest firearm-trained persons to serve in the zoo, I have no doubt that that will be surpassed at some time in the near future or maybe already has.

The keepers who took on the task had to right from the very beginning realise that the day could come where they could be faced with the reality of shooting one of the animals that they cared for. Most of the shooting crew originated from the carnivore department and we would every couple of months or so go down to a local rifle range to get in some shooting practice. The zoo would also conduct dry runs where we would go through the process of a dangerous animal escaping and then have a briefing as to how we believed it all panned out. At one time there was no real roster in place and the zoo would rely on a trained keeper to rally to the call if needed. At times I found myself being the only firearm keeper on duty.

After some years a curator proposed the idea across of passing on the duties to the police, I was completely against this for the reasons I have already explained. I then set to work writing a long, detailed memo as to why we should maintain trained keepers as Firearm Personnel. After long discussions, considerations, and debating, the decision was made by management to continue the program within the zoo, much to the relief of all of us as we knew that to pass it on to another body would be full of problems and other issues.

So it was decided at that point to review the whole system and make some important changes. One was to have more licensed Firearm Personnel and those who wished to take on the task would as well as us be put through fitness, medical and psychological analysis testing. One Senior Keeper on the department had a significant heart issue diagnosed during this process and received the appropriate treatment. Also that Firearm Personnel would receive an allowance calculated into their fortnightly pay. The first thing that came to mind for me was that it had to be more than the money but something that would be valuable to the staff and zoo management, and the animals in the collection. Eventually we had a final group of people selected from various departments who wished to take on the testing and training, we all went through the agreed system. We selected a firearm trainer at a rifle range who put us through our paces, and she evaluated us to ensure very high standards were met. Some keepers decided that it wasn't for them as they had difficulty with the process, but that was ok by the group as that's what the intensive training programme was all about. No one had any negative feelings towards them, they had given it a go and that's more than anyone could ask of them. At one time one of the managers came up with the idea of presenting old zoo trophies he had found in the Board Room, to be presented to the best shooters. We were all good at what we did, and I soon convinced him that this was not a competition and should never be considered to be one. We would take the opportunity to not only be under the watchful eye of a firearm trainer but to also avail ourselves of facilities at some shooting ranges so we could improve and sharpen our own skills.

The system worked very well indeed and was a result of a team built on trust and respect. The attitude that we all took was that it was not a matter of if, but a matter of when an animal would escape, and it was important to keep that in mind.

The time did come one afternoon when I was the rostered Firearm Person. One of the Orangutans had broken through the exhibit wire and was enjoying the city views from the top of the enclosure. Orangutans are dangerous, their sheer strength and intelligence makes them so. With a firearm in hand after being transported through the zoo to the Orangutan exhibit, myself and another primate keeper were confronted with the male Orangutan. The keeper on the scene was quick on his feet and had a bag full of walnuts in his possession which he threw into the now isolated and secured public viewing area. The Orangutan, after summing it up, decided that the walnuts were a better option than interacting with us. The keeper managed to eventually hand-inject him through a wire grill with an anaesthetic and render him harmless. Orangutans were trained to present their shoulders for such a procedure eliminating any stress to them. He was safely returned to his rightful place after his escape route had been repaired.

I can also remember that fateful day on the 13th of July 2013, as Firearm Person again for the day I was called up to the off-limit Gorilla complex as Rigo, our 42-year-old Gorilla, had suffered a heart attack within one of the off-limit facilities. Rigo had been reintegrated into the Gorilla group sometime before, sharing the enclosure with five females. He had in the past shown aggressive behaviour which created difficulties in managing the group, however he was eventually integrated successfully back within the group. Rigo came to the zoo with a young female Gorilla, Yuska, in 1972. Rigo's death was sudden, and while the vets frantically made every effort to revive him, it was to no avail. The grief that I shared with the staff was very distressing. So sad that such a Melbourne Zoo icon had passed away and before many Primate Keepers' eyes. I am so fortunate to this very day that I was never put in a situation that I had to shoot an escaped animal, and I have always put this down to the excellent safety and work practices at the zoo.

Fox on the Run

The urban fox lives amongst us, being most active at night and in the early hours of the morning. They have been declared a pest after being introduced into Australia in the 1850s. They are found in all mainland states and territories and can adapt very well in all types of environments from Alpine areas to rainforests.

There was at one time a fox getting into the zoo grounds overnight. It had killed several species of small native mammals. The staff was asked to not only be on the lookout, but to make sure that perimeter gates were fully closed upon their departure at the end of the working day. The local supplier of our sheep was employed by management to catch the fox, this involved him coming in after hours, and check for any fox activity and setting traps or possibly shooting the intruder at no risk to any other animals or staff. His fee for this service was $1000 and he was for some unknown reason paid in full prior to the capture of the fox. Mr Fox Catcher would appear on the property around 5pm every evening and would set traps around certain areas of the zoo. One evening as I was preparing to head for home he asked me if I would set the traps for him, a task that would take some hours. I asked him what he would be prepared to pay me for the off duty out of hours work. He expected me to offer my services to him free of charge, but I firmly rejected this request. It was several days later when a call came over the radio that the fox had been sighted down near the hay sheds at the back of the zoo. Within minutes I arrived at the location with a rifle in hand. Within several minutes I could hear keepers in hot pursuit of the fox, and as it ran past me I shot it. It was not a fatal shot, so it was still mobile, but quickly caught up in a net and several minutes later it died. On arriving at the curator's office I informed them that the fox had not only been shot but captured as well. No doubt everyone was relieved however I believe that Mr Fox Catcher was not asked to return the $1000.

Another fox rampaged through the little Penguin Exhibit one night in 2015, killing 14 of the 29 little penguins. The fox returned to the scene the following evening and was picked up on CCTV cameras. Traps had already been set as well and positioned around the zoo. The 15 surviving penguins had been moved to a more secure area. A fox controller was employed to track the intruder, and attempts were made to fox proof the main gates. No fox to my knowledge was caught.

A Stint at Werribee

Victoria's Open Range Zoo was established in Werribee in 1975 and is part of Zoos Victoria along with Healesville Sanctuary, and of course Melbourne Zoo. It was opened to the public in 1983. It consists of 200 hectares with open grasslands featuring animals from Africa, including giraffes, rhinos, lions and hippos, and from America such as the American bison. Also included are Australian marsupials such as emus and kangaroos. At that time it was home to some 360 animals of 40 species.

To enable one of the Werribee, or Victorias Open Range zookeepers to get some carnivore keeping experience I did a keeper exchange with him for three months. This involved quite a considerable amount of travelling by car, some 51 km with an overall round trip of over 100 km per day, and as it was in the middle of winter, I had to prepare myself by wearing double insulated clothing under my zoo uniform to protect myself from the bitter cold mornings. This was a very wise move as this apparel came in handy when I found myself on freezing frosty mornings pushing out bales of hay in the open paddocks from the open tray food truck. We would sometimes toss for it as it was always preferable to be in the truck's cabin driving with the heater on of course, but I got my fair share of that. It was always entertaining to watch a herd of bison or buffalo chasing the truck as you off loaded their breakfast, and if the truck stopped you would be surrounded by them, a daunting experience from the back of the tray truck.

Most mornings upon arriving early to beat the usual peak hour traffic I would get the opportunity to take my rifle out to the uninhabited areas of the zoo and shoot the many rabbits that frequented the open paddocks, providing fresh food for the cats.

It was great to work with many animal species and other keepers that I had not had an opportunity of working with before, and also to pass on my knowledge in some areas. Even though I enjoyed the open spaces and working with different people, I was glad to get back to Melbourne Zoo, with some valuable experiences under my belt. The exchange keeper wanted to extend his stay at Melbourne Zoo but the extensive amount of travelling for me had become a major factor and I had other projects that I wished to attend to back at Melbourne Zoo.

Stormy Times

In 1998 a huge cyclonic storm ripped through Melbourne Zoo tearing down branches, fences, and numerous trees. Being called into the Zoo in the early hours of the morning was very unsettling, not knowing which carnivores may or may not have escaped. Luckily only some birds found temporary freedom and were returned to their enclosures safely. The zoo for the only time in its recorded history at this time, was closed for the whole day, with the constant sounds of chainsaws heard throughout the property. It took some weeks to eventually clear all the debris and torn down trees from the grounds.

Keys to the Zoo

Every evening on the weekends when I was the designated Senior Animal Keeper, the zoo master keys would religiously have to be returned to the key lock up at the end of every working day, so they could be accessed by staff the following day. It had been a long week and weekend with big crowds, and I finished much later than usual due to a number of issues needing my attention. I was tired, hungry and looking forward to several well-earned days off. Driving home on a Sunday wasn't all that easy with still plenty of cars around with people leaving the zoo or the nearby football ground, most still enjoying what was left of the weekend. It would take me just on an hour to get home to Eltham. The traffic was heavier and slower than usual. My usual work take home keys always hung on my right side from a clip on my belt and I for some reason reached down to untangle one of them and soon realised that I had forgotten to return the master key, resulting in a U-turn and a trip back to the zoo, where the traffic was even heavier. From that day it was a lesson learnt that would prevent me from using more petrol than I had to.

Lock checking at the end of the day was always a priority and I would methodically go over each padlock to ensure that everything was secure either for me or someone else who was to work the round the following day. One night after the evening meal I had an uneasy feeling that I had not properly checked an off-limit snake-holding unit in the Education Facility. After attempting to go to sleep I realised that there was only one way to put an end to my concerns and that was to drive back to the zoo and check it. It was as you could well imagine an easy drive at that time of night and my worries were quickly dispelled as everything was indeed secured.

Oh and that's not all folks. I misplaced my car keys one evening after a Zoo Twilight Concert and after much searching had to call my wife to come and pick me up. With arrangements made the following morning for a company to come into the zoo and issue me with a new set keys, at great expense I might add, only to find them in the Carnivore Office behind a kettle.

On Par with the Carnivores

Several holes of the Royal Park Golf Course ran parallel to the zoo wall and on many occasions wayward golf balls would come sailing over the zoo wall, ending up in various carnivore enclosures or find an unsuspecting target such as a keeper going about their duties. One keeper was struck on the back of the head, luckily it didn't do much damage apart from some bruising. Staff would inevitably remove them from where they lay in certain areas, and over several years some four large buckets were full of these missiles. On clearing up an off-limit area I came across the overflowing buckets and decided to finally get rid of them and put them to good use, offering them back to the Golf Club where they came from, for a price. The financial gain was spent on sustaining the Carnivore Department with coffee, tea and biscuits for many months. I was interviewed on a radio station regarding this practice and apparently the host of the show called me a capitalist, for which I believe she received some re buffing from her listeners.

To Sweep or not to Sweep

Every afternoon at 4.30pm several members of the Carnivore Department would close off the public pathway which ran in front of the Big Cat Complex. This was referred to as 'sweeping the area', to ensure that no members of the public were in the area at 5pm closing time. Once done we would radio into the department that the sweep was completed. While most visitors complied there were always the few who refused to exit the area and would confront zoo staff. While we understood how some may have felt, we also kept in mind that they had had all day to view the big cats, and that this was a safety-first procedure. Some visitors would disclose to you that they had arrived at the zoo at 4 pm and wanted to get their money's worth, maybe they should have arrived at opening time to achieve that. Keeping in mind that there was only a ribbon barrier preventing anyone from entering, some surely did after we had gone. One major issue with the sweep process was the public address system, as every evening around 4.45pm the receptionist would make the announcement for the visitors to please make their way to the exits as the zoo was due to close. Within seconds of this announcement the lions would begin to roar, attracting what visitors remained to their enclosure. There were several occasions that I was threatened with bodily harm if I did not allow them to view the cats. This also became a problem for many staff members on the department, but it was something that we had to contend with. It also presented the same issues with the twilight crowds. Apart from all this we also had to make sure that all the rubbish bin lids were secured and locked to prevent the resident possums from getting into them overnight.

The Carnivore Office

This was situated at the end of the Big Cat Complex and was more like a bunker in appearance. It had a window in the wall we shared with an off-limit yard, with a bench just below it, so when the big cat was sitting on it, it got a firsthand view of us all, maybe viewing us like sardines in a can. It was amazing how we fitted so much into such a small space with chairs, a desk, a sink and gun cabinet as well as shelves for reference books and paperwork, even a television on the wall. We managed somehow to coexist in relative harmony with one another. We had an area outside where we could sit and eat on warm days, but on cold ones it was standing room only inside. It had a flat concrete roof, and it was our intention at one stage to have steps or a ladder leading up to the roof so we could have more room and an upstairs lounge area. This eventually changed and after years of being in such a small office a prefabbed one was installed just opposite with much more space and room for the ever-expanding staff levels. The bunker office still stands today as a storage shed.

Are They Out There?

Television news reports would often cover the subject of big cat sightings around the countryside. Farmers, campers, hikers and others coming across what appeared to be an exotic cat roaming amongst the vegetation. A file was put together by the Carnivore Department documenting all such sightings. In one year there were some 38 big cat sightings. Feral cats can grow to around 40 to 60 cm and weigh 3.6 kg or more. They are predominantly short haired individuals with coat colours ranging from ginger to grey, striped or black. In one case a feral cat weighing 6.8 kg was captured on Morton Island, and prior to its capture had been called the Tangalooma Puma, so one could understand why there were so many cases of mistaken identity. I eventually took on the task of sorting, collating and taking reports into a file that we could refer to. Reports of pumas or panthers sighted crossing the road were numerous, and in reading the reports one thing stood out as common, that these big cats were observed by locals while coming home from long drinking sessions at the local hotel, sometimes at one or two in the morning. One so-called sighting reported seeing a black jaguar sitting by the side of a road with a sheep in its mouth. Nevertheless we took all reports on board.

Some reports had an element of interest while others were proved by the witness of a cat sighting bringing in a plaster cast of the footprint. On every occasion one could see that it belonged to a dog due to the claws being visible, cats have retractable claws which would not show up in a cast. Some farmers would visit me with photos, and a story of his or her sightings. These were photos that were not connected in any way, but the result of the farmer putting it all together, for example a wombat burrow and some faeces nearby, with a sheep carcass in the creek a few meters away. The burrow would be presumed to be the cat's den and of course it had defecated nearby and the carcass, the remains of its latest meal. Facts once presented were always somewhat disappointing to the bearer. An exotic cat does not dig a den, or use a burrow to reside in. They would stay out of sight under heavy undergrowth and stay away from human habitation. It would cover its faeces and not tear a sheep apart. Usually upon closer investigation the carcass in question had been in the creek for a considerable length of time with its death being due to some other reason. Presenting the facts would always bring about some other reason or explanation by the farmer or landowner as to why there is a cat other than a domestic one on their property.

News and television reports concerning such sightings would sometimes bring a plethora of comments from people claiming they too had seen such an animal even though they lived in another state. One section of video footage showed a black cat of considerable size approaching a kangaroo who stood her ground, standing erect and displaying protective behaviours as she had pouch young. The cat kept its distance and eventually moved on. When viewing the footage, questions were raised as to the way in which the cat moved and looked exactly like a domestic cat, it was large no doubt, but feral domestic cats can attain a considerable size. I've seen them in the bush and been impressed by the size that some of them can reach. The kangaroo I believe would not have stayed around by natural instinct alone if it had been confronted by an exotic cat. And so we would evaluate every sighting by the pure process of what we knew and saw by a process of elimination. Often members of the Australian Rare Fauna Research Association would pay us a visit with footage which we would confirm was a feral cat and not an exotic one. The Association was formed in 1984 and has collated thousands of reports and sightings of animals resembling Pumas, Panthers and even Tasmanian Tigers.

One phone call was transferred to me from a woman in the country who informed me of her experiences with exotic cats, and that she had without a word of doubt had Pumas on her back decking on several evenings, roaring and causing a considerable amount of noise and panic amongst her livestock. She paused at the end of it inviting me and a film crew to visit her property one evening to witness the event. I then proceeded to inform her that in fact Pumas do not roar due to the very structure of certain bones in their throat, and due to this they are not classified as a big cat, but the largest species of the small cat family. My informative reply was followed by the hanging up of the phone from her end.

While visiting the zoo a farmer informed me that he frequently came across exotic big cats on his property and could easily shoot one anytime he felt that way inclined. I asked him if he could describe the cat to me, which resulted in a textbook description of a Black Panther. He was aware of the story that the USA armed forces had released several Black Panthers into the bush at the end of the war. This was all speculation, and he believed they were the very animals still roaming the countryside. "How long has it been since the end of WW2? And how long do panthers live for?" was my reply. If they happened to be the offspring of the original pair, if they were a pair and compatible then maybe it would be worth his while to shoot them, to prove the issues once and for all. I never heard from him again and to this day he probably believes that they are still around. I'm not one to argue with that.

We never ridiculed anyone who approached us with a sighting, and yes I believe that species of exotic cats can survive within an Australian bush environment, but they have specific behaviours. They don't make their presence obvious; they hide their faeces, and would move around quietly during the night or early morning or evening. They would stay away from roads, certainly not run across the road in front of cars, and they don't tear sheep or cows to pieces as most people would think they do as they have specific eating habits. And so the list goes on. I'm sure the zoo will not hear the end of it as there are people who are determined not to allow the facts to get in the way of a good story. As far as I'm concerned I firmly believe that the theory is well and truly yet to be proved, and who knows maybe one day it might be proven that they are out there.

CHAPTER 11

On to Primates

I was given the opportunity to make a move onto the Primate Department. Working with large primates was always a challenge, as they were always looking at ways of getting to you, or at you at any time. Rigo our male silverback Gorilla would bang on the metal shute door so hard and fast that the Gorilla off-limit area would vibrate and echo so loudly you would have to almost leave the area with your ears ringing. Rigo's claim to fame was that he was the father of Mazuri, the world's first Gorilla born by artificial insemination in 1984, a year before I started at the zoo. Mazuri, or Ya Kwanza as he was called by members of the primate staff, meaning The First. I had the glorious opportunity, in 1993, to spend a considerable amount of time in with Mazuri, yes *in* with him and we played some games and held onto one another. This was a sad moment as he was due to be sent overseas to Jersey Wildlife Preservation Trust to be incorporated into their group as the head breeding male Gorilla. Years later Mazuri was transferred to a zoo in France and passed away at 32 years of age. He was one of the most iconic Gorillas from Melbourne Zoo. I miss him to this day and will never forget the precious time I have spent with him.

One of the young Orangutans would hang on the wire of the off-limit den and wait for you or visiting groups to get close enough for him to shove his penis out through the wire. Some Orangutans would wear or walk around with hessian bags on them as if they were on a fashion parade. Some would use them to beat any unfortunate possum that had made its way into the dens. They were always on guard to surprise you in some way or another. Some would bring in sticks they had collected from their enclosure, and they would take great pleasure in using them to get the fluorescent lights that hung by chains in the off-limit areas in the passageway, swinging back and forward, almost to the stage that they would be smashed against the wire. Upon us coming in to investigate they would hide their sticks and assume a 'don't look at me' attitude. At times they would use their sticks to poke at us as we walked by.

One morning after cleaning one of the Orangutan's exhibits and letting the primate out into the display, the keeper realised that he had left his rake inside the enclosure. On running out to the front there sat the Orangutan with the said rake in her hand. Keepers with a box full of bananas made it clear to the primate that if she returned the rake, she would be rewarded with a banana or two. In looking at the item that the keepers wished her to return, she proceeded to break up the rake into pieces and managed to get half of the contents of the banana box by trading for it, piece by piece. Needless to say that the rake as evidence of the primate's intelligence was swiftly discarded. In the1980s an Orangutan named Ken at San Diego zoo escaped his enclosure and walked down public pathways stopping to look at other animals as if he was a visitor. A few weeks later he escaped again. Zookeepers found him in front of another ape enclosure throwing rocks at Otis, a fellow Orangutan and former pen mate, who according to the records was not known to be amiable. The escapes continued with Ken using a crowbar that workers had left behind he tossed it to another Orangutan who used it to pry open a window and let Ken out. Kens escape attempts were eventually foiled by the installation of an electric fence in his enclosure. Orangutans will find and work on some area that interests them and take on the challenge over time to eventually work out how to loosen or remove an object that may very well give them some freedom.

The zoo's Chimpanzees would each receive a tin of condensed milk, and it was the job of the smartest female in the group to gather up the tins once empty, and return them via the safety shute to the keeper. During a Zoo Directors conference and while on a tour of the Ape Facility, the group came upon one of the head keepers drenched, screaming at one of the chimps to return the tins and stop spitting milk at him. In pure rage and frustration the keeper threw the remains of the milk from bucket at the chimps who were delighted with the opportunity to lick the milk from their bodies. A comment was made to the group that sometimes keepers just had a bad day. It was always interesting and a challenge to work with primates who share with humans a high percentage of their DNA.

Working every second weekend meant that we would not always be able to go to the footy to watch our favourite team play, when it came to finals we could sometimes swap weekends or days so we could attend a finals game. With my team being in a Grand Final I couldn't get anyone to swap the day with me so I had to work. My game plan was to start early, work through morning tea and lunch to see my way clear to watch the game on one of the Ape House television sets. We had several of them operating in the morning to entertain the Gorillas. So with the work behind me I ventured into the Ape House to watch the game, and there in front of one of the televisions was a chair with a side table with some freshly cooked popcorn. Needless to say that my team lost but the kind thought made it a little less painful.

The Pits

The old Gorilla, Chimpanzee and Orangutan pits were built in 1974, a positive move away from concrete and steel fronted cages. Although they provided some more space for the primates, they fell short when it came to arboreal space for the Orangutans, leaving no real areas for escape from the public eyes. Rigo, the resident silverback Gorilla, managed to on some occasions defecate in his hand and throw it in frustration at the public, sometimes changing his ammunition to stones, or clods of dirt, on one occasion narrowly missing a visitor with a rock. The surface of the pits were made of a rough form of concrete, and one had to venture down to the very bottom of each pit to remove any faeces, also shredded paper and other items that were used for enrichment for the primates. This meant dragging several wheelie bins down and straining against the weight of them when pulling them back up from the bottom. Not exactly a good way to operate. Then one would have to drag the heavy-duty hose down and completely wash down the surface before cleaning each adjoining drain. It was a long, wet, arduous stressful and at times dangerous job, that could take sometimes hours to complete depending on the amount of material and bedding that had been taken into the enclosure by the inhabitants the day before, no one on the department enjoyed it and everyone was totally exhausted after completing the task, but we all accepted the fact that it had to be done without question for the benefit of the primates. Much later a company was employed to train staff to use a harness system to prevent anyone falling into the pits or injuring themselves but this proved to be so time consuming and expensive that other safety measures were adopted. Thankfully these old pits no longer exist, but the memories of cleaning them still linger.

Breakout at the Top Six

Previously the old Baboon area was divided into six sections, containing various species of primates from Mandrills to Capuchin Monkeys. Capuchins are a species from South America and are considered one of the most intelligent.

One of the males in the group was called Erwin and would always get excited on seeing an approaching keeper. One fateful day the cage door was left unlocked, and all the capuchin monkeys made their way onto the top of their cage. As the back wall of the top six enclosures was the front wall of the zoo, there was great concern that the troop would jump over it and make good their escape into the surrounding parklands. Erwin however was the only monkey to think of that, and as the rest of the capuchins rushed back inside their cage, Erwin made a dash for his freedom, with several primate keepers in hot pursuit. One keeper, with net in hand, approached a man lying on a park bench and asked him if he had seen the escapee. "Monkey?" replied the man, "I thought it was a possum." Erwin proved to be too agile and elusive and keepers failed to locate him. However around 4pm that afternoon the zoo received a call from a North Melbourne resident informing them that there was a monkey in the backyard. It didn't take long for adventurous Erwin to be caught up and returned to his home in the zoo. It is today the only mass breakout recorded at the zoo. It is noted in earlier publications that the zoo first acquired several Capuchin Monkeys from a sailor around 1900s.

Another primate escapee involved a Chacma Baboon that made his way into a local residence and got through the bathroom window, and I believe the bathroom was occupied at the time. He was soon recaptured and returned to his enclosure.

Baboons on the Move

I spent several years on this department and the main project I coordinated with a fellow keeper was the moving of the Baboons to their new enclosure. We had at the time some sixteen Hamadryas Baboons. They represented one of the five species of Baboons, with wild populations found in Ethiopia, Somalia, and Saudi Arabia. At night they congregate on cliff tops for protection, coming down at sunrise to search for food such as seeds, plants and even small mammals. They can live to a ripe old age of some 37 years and live in extensive groups called troops with a dominant male as the leader and protector.

We had at the top end of the zoo a 40-square-metre Hamadryas Baboon enclosure which at one time had been divided up to house up to six species of primates, and also at one time Eurasian Badgers. It was then known or referred to by keeping staff as 'the top six'. Many stories exist of episodes that occurred with this facility, including a whole group of Capuchin Monkeys being accidentally let out, as I have previously mentioned, one of which found its way into the nearby parklands surrounding the zoo. Or some keepers failing to secure locks or doors, then finding themselves in with a troop of primates. The whole area was eventually set aside to house the sixteen Baboons, and although made up of concrete and wire, the area was furnished with rocks and some large logs and branches. The Baboons also had night dens that they could escape into. The whole area was cold in winter and hot in summer and was indeed an area that was almost as old as the zoo itself and proved to be very popular with the visitors.

Management had from time to time raised the issue of relocating the Baboon troop, one option was moving them to the Open Range Zoo at Werribee. As I was working the round at the time, a colleague and I decided to visit the then director whom we knew well, to discuss an alternative new enclosure for them. Putting across the fact that the Baboon group was the largest group of primates within Melbourne Zoo's collection, and that the public spent a considerable amount of time at the enclosure, being fascinated by their behaviour, and we firmly believed that the zoo had an obligation to keep them. We presented other issues that supported this reasoning, and we had thought the process through carefully before presenting our case. Our case over time was given due consideration and the outcome was that the Melbourne Zoo would continue to keep the Baboon troop, with a plan to build a new spacious enclosure for them in the future, which became Baboon Lookout.

Some several years later it was decided that a new exhibit would be built at the back section of the zoo, taking over old real estate that once housed several species of deer. It would be 2,000 square meters in size, with several spacious off-limit areas both inside and out. As I was still working primates at the time, I was involved in the project planning group that would meet from time to time to discuss details of the new facility and had the opportunity to have major input into its size, shape and design. Over the following months the concept was completed, and it was rather exciting to see the whole thing take shape, knowing that it was going to be a state-of-the-art exhibit in Australia for Baboons.

Several people were involved in the meetings ranging from architects, interpretation signage, and keeping staff to public relations, all knowing that their involvement would be required as the project proceeded.

My task was not only having input as to the husbandry requirements, but the training of the Baboons in readiness for the move day. The coordination of the catch up would take up the whole day. This involved having a right-hand man, someone who knew the Baboons as well as I did and could support and assist in the project. One close colleague and friend was selected for this task as he was outstanding in his work and was more than capable of standing in for me on my rostered days off.

The old exhibit had two sections, the small and large side, this was used to move the Baboons from one end to the other when servicing the enclosure. The small side had an off-limit race at the back where the Baboons could be secured from the rest of the exhibit in the event of segregating an individual Baboon for treatment etc. With the installation of a new shute door the Baboons could be let into this back area from the large side and isolated.

Baboons however are smarter than most people give them credit for, and not all sixteen would venture into the area at once, so a training plan was written up. The Baboons would be run into the area to get their food, positive reinforcement so to speak, which proved successful. Over the weeks all the Baboons would move into this area without any stress or complications.

As the time drew nearer we had to look at how we could get all the Baboons into this area on the day without food. Whenever an animal is to be taken to the vets for a procedure, or it is to be caught up its stomach needs to be void of food to prevent any major complications. The answer came in the form of paper bags. We offered the Baboons their food in paper bags scattered around the off-limit area. They soon accepted this as the norm and would get rather excited at the sight of any bag that a keeper had in his or her possession. However on moving day the bags would contain no food at all. As the new exhibit neared completion other departments became more involved, such as public relations, to discuss how the media was to be involved, and when the press releases would be issued. Opening date was scheduled just before the September school holidays. As almost always happens, a delay cropped up, with the treatment of some of the steel work preventing this due date from happening. Interpretation signage plays an important part of any display, providing the visitors with information on the species. The interpretation manager was rather put out by this delay, as everyone else was, including myself. When a new display or exhibit is built there needs to be a window of time to allow the animals to settle into their new environs. This can take up to several weeks. Baboons are no exception to this and on the opening day with the media one would want all the animals to come out of their off-limit areas and into the enclosure. Unknown to the media and public this was something that they had been doing for some time previously and it was just a normal routine for the Baboons. I suggested to the rather annoyed interpretation manager that some boxes that had been made up to move the Baboons could be placed in front of the Baboon Exhibit, and we could inform the public as part of our daily Baboon presentation how we were to move the animals and promote the new display, thus making the most of a delayed situation. So this unexpected delay gave us time to allow the visitors to see how we manage our animals when it came to moving them, and we incorporated this into our daily Baboon talks.

The primate staff and keepers from other divisions were invited to have some input into the moving day schedule and they each had a part to play. There were two plans in place in case one did not work we would have something to fall back on. Each keeper involved was given a timetable and schedule time sheet and would be required to present themselves at the old enclosure at a certain time. The plan was to run all Baboons into the off-limit race, then separate the larger males and restrain them, sending them to the vets for a full health check-up, then transport them to the off-limit area of the new display. They were to be processed first so as to avoid them becoming stressed at watching the other members of the group being caught up and removed. Then the remaining Baboons would be put through the same process. A keeper would be stationed at the new exhibit to assist releasing the Baboons and observing them.

Everything ran as planned and all the Baboons were caught up and run through the procedure without any issues. The whole routine had taken some twelve hours, and we all stood in the new spacious keeper off-limit area observing the Baboons exploring their new home.

The Baboons had spent many years in the most exposed area of the zoo, with public and staff going past, not to mention the noises of traffic and nocturnal sounds, both natural and human, coming over the fence `from the adjoining car park. As the off-limit area was roofed it became immediately obvious that the Baboons were making alarm calls if anything landed on the roof, such as a bird or something falling from a tree. They were constantly looking up at the roof in anticipation of another noise that they would bark at as Baboons do when they become aggressive of stressed. Over beer and pizza to celebrate the successful move we observed this behaviour over and over again, and I decided that it would be beneficial for me to stay overnight to observe them. My faithful right-hand man kept me company. The following morning, after a somewhat restless night we had spent sleeping on hay bales, all Baboons eventually settled and enjoyed a bonus breakfast of their favourite food items.

After some time the Baboons were given full access to the exhibit. Following the dominant male the troop stopped at the outside off-limit yard door, which they had access to, and looked out into a vast area they had never seen previously. They all backed away and alarm barked, there was no wire above them, something they felt most uncomfortable with. As each day passed the troop made further inroads into the main area and within a week were completely comfortable and settled, moving with ease through the display. One issue that concerned the zoo gardeners was the accessibility that the Baboons had to the planted areas. A hot wire system was installed to protect the foliage. I had major concerns with this system that it would not be adequate enough to keep the Baboons at bay, and time proved me right as the younger Baboons could get under the base wire. It was eventually changed after some damage to several plants. On the official opening day invited guests and the media were a witness to a spectacular Baboon troop running out to feed on display. The Chairman of the Board was most impressed, not that he knew that we had been rehearsing this for some weeks prior to the opening. I'm so honoured to have played a part in such a major project, giving the zoo's troop of Baboons a new home. To this day they are breeding very successfully, which is what Baboon society is all about. Sometime later a morning tea function was held at the old Baboon exhibit for all staff to get the opportunity to have a graffiti session, which proved to be a very popular event prior to the area being demolished. All in all the Baboon move project was one of the most satisfying projects I've ever been involved with.

A Moment of Freedom

A female Orangutan managed with the aid of some large bamboo plants which had blown over during the day, to make good her escape over the moat. I was in servicing a small primate cage directly opposite her escape point. The procedure for animal escapes was to stay away from the immediate area, and if possible keep indoors until you were called, or the animal had been captured and returned to its rightful place. As I was within a caged area, I stayed put and observed the Orangutan knocking over rubbish bins, as she made her way along the public viewing pathway. I kept everyone informed of her exact location. One of the horticulture staff was parked on a tractor just outside the cage I was in, and as the Orangutan approached him and proceeded to climb onto the tractor he attempted to push her away. As Orangutans are incredibly strong she was not perturbed in spite of my warnings to allow her to do what she wanted the staff member continued to attempt to push her away resulting in a rather severe bite to his leg.

After some time however the Orangutan decided that it was all a bit too much and made her way back into her enclosure after her favourite food was thrown over the moat. The Orangutan was OK following the incident but the same could not be said for the unfortunate horticultural member who spent a considerable amount of time in hospital recovering from a very nasty and deep bite wound.

Many years prior the other significant Orangutan escapee was an Orangutan housed in those days in one of the enclosures on the main drive, now no longer in use but preserved as a representation of old zoo enclosures. When the call went out that the Orangutan was on the loose, several senior animal staff members were soon on the scene. The escapee then approached one of them, climbing onto him and began to lift his shirt followed by several kisses. By the time they got back to the scene of the crime the Orangutan had by this time firmly attached itself to its chosen carer. It took several of them to entice it off and even as they walked it back into the enclosure it still had a good secure hold on his leg wanting to invite him in. Fortunately they were both successfully separated and could go their own separate ways.

CHAPTER 12

Back in the Pool

At one time I found myself back on the Marine Mammal Department, which at the time had undergone a complete change of staff. My main involvement was with seal training and seal presentations, with the relatively new crew. I also got involved with the training of Storm, a male seal destined for Taronga Zoo. In order for his departure to be successful, and with minimal stress for Storm, we were training him to become familiar with the shipment container. This involved leaving it with him when he was off display and encouraging him to sit in it or on it with a positive reward of fish. Once we and he had achieved this, we were able to get him into his shipment box on moving day.

As the seal exhibit was ageing, we had to replace or repair some underground gate valves. We were able, as a cost saving, to perform some of this ourselves, although it wasn't the preferred way as far as I was concerned as it involved a lot of heavy work, that should have been outsourced. However the task was completed and the areas that had been dug up were re cemented and the mock rock work was repainted.

The department was teamed with the elephant section, and we would be running from one section to the other cleaning up copious amounts of elephant dung in the Elephant House and feeding seals as well as doing all the seal feeding presentations. It just was not for me, and I felt that the marriage between the departments was not working all that well. I then transferred back to primates and after a short time there, moved back to carnivores. It had gone through a number of changes as well. It was to be the last department I would work on before I my departure to the other side of the wall.

CHAPTER 13

Enrichment and Training

Within some type of confined space, enrichment is a necessity to give animals some link with their environment and to overcome boredom. Meat would be offered in large tyres, or tied down so considerable effort from the animal was required to release it. Food was hidden or scattered around the enclosure to promote foraging behaviours. On hot days large ice blocks were placed around the exhibit with meat or fruit frozen into it. Some animals were given access to their night dens and yards where it was considerably cooler. On one occasion Mount Buller Ski Resort generously transported truckloads of snow down to the zoo which was placed in many enclosures to stimulate the inhabitants. Small kiddie wading pools were used, as well as cardboard tubes stuffed with shredded paper or nuts. Plastic balls, ropes, and cardboard boxes full of treats were all used. Timetables were set up as to what to offer different carnivores, so as not to fall into some kind or routine and to keep activities different. It was also a good practice to observe the outcomes of the enrichment programs, and to change things if it wasn't working or could be improved in some way. The only disadvantage with this was that it did make the enclosures look untidy, but good interpretation signage was later installed, to inform visitors about enrichment.

As I was a member of the Bromeliad Society of Victoria I arranged for members to bring in their surplus plants to place in some South American exhibits. The response was amazing with a number of members coming in with trailer loads of bromeliads. So with armfuls of these amazing colourful plants, we managed to place them in a number of areas with all of the inhabitants being stimulated by them. Some small primates peering inside their leaves for any insect treats to eat. It was the best enrichment program that I have been involved with. Even after I had left the zoo the Bromeliad Society has continued with these most generous donations.

I've seen training of some animals where the focus appears to be on the trainer, with exaggerated movements and getting the animal to behave in some human like manner. Training should, I believe, be to allow the animal in question to behave naturally. Training is also of utmost use and importance when it comes down to administering medication or injections, such as primates presenting their shoulder at the wire so as they can be injected. Positive reinforcement is always used; that is to ignore the negative behaviours and reward the positive ones. It also reinforces the keeper animal relationship, strengthening trust and bonding between the two.

CHAPTER 14

Parkville Pranks

We would from time to time take it upon ourselves to provide some relief from the pressures of the job and partake in a little bit of Parkville pranks.

One of the earliest pranks that has always been regarded as a classic was the situation where a new keeper, who was rather apprehensive when it came to snakes, was given the task of looking after one. Even though this keeper was not on the Reptile Department, he did not question the tasks so as to give a good impression. Day to day he would cautiously clean the snake's abode and place a deceased mouse in the tank, even though he detested the task, he persevered without complaint. This went on for a considerable amount of time until one day the truth of the whole matter was revealed. The enclosure housed a Rubber Snake, which was also attended secretly by another staff member who would move the rubber snake around, remove the mouse, and place in some fresh snake faeces, of course giving the unsuspecting new keeper the impression that the snake was indeed very much alive and consuming his offerings.

Another prank, that involved animal faeces, was upon completing many years on one department and going to another I was presented with a gift. A tin of what appeared to be full of chocolate truffles covered in coconut, when if fact it was balls of wombat faeces covered in coconut. On another occasion a birthday cake was discovered to be a large square of foam rubber covered in icing. Fortunately none of these items were consumed or attempted to be consumed.

During one April Fool's Day morning a native mammal keeper completely emptied the Native Mammal Office, known as the Humpy, of all furniture and fittings prior to staff coming back from morning smoko, who were shocked to find the Humpy totally bare. The items were later found stored in an off-limit shed.

The same keeper was involved in one of the best all time pranks ever carried out within the zoo. It had been reported that there was from time to time a rather suspiciously behaving character carrying a plastic bag within the zoo grounds. Keepers and ground staff would encounter him on occasion with one staff member who he followed into the toilets where he was heard making loud grunting and guttural noises in the adjoining cubicle. It did not take long before this individual was the talk of the zoo, turning up unexpectedly around the grounds at various times scaring the hell out of staff. One morning while a large proportion of us were having morning tea at the Native Mammal Office, the grunting stranger appeared out of nowhere with a large stick in his hand. As he approached, some keepers quickly scattered while one of the staff member decided to take him on, weapon and all. It didn't take long in the following struggle to realise that it was all pre-staged and the stranger soon took off his wig and other disguises to reveal himself much to the relief of the onlookers. One individual was utterly amazed at the effects of the prank, stating that someone should have recorded it all. One point of the finger revealed a staff member on the roof of the office filming the whole event.

On returning from days off the Keeper in Charge of Marine Mammals found his desk, phone and files placed outside on display amongst the rocks. As he didn't really like to acknowledge other people's pranks, he walked out onto the display, sat down at his desk and proceeded to do some paperwork at usual.

While the electricians were wiring up some new off-limit reptile holding boxes some stirring and bantering was going on. It got to the stage that just as one of the sparkies was getting into one of the large lower boxes to wire it up as it was quite large, enough to accommodate a large python, one of the keepers placed a live rat in with him, which as you could imagine resulted in much screaming and banging.

Another old tale told of keepers placing fly pupae in a Director's desk drawer with some fresh otter faeces which resulted in the office becoming plagued with masses of newly hatched flies.

A shop window dummy was used in front of the back off-limit areas housing some species that would need to get accustomed to staff being around. It was a good conditioning practice. The dummy would appear in the most unlikely places, scaring the intended victim, turning him or her into a nervous wreck.

Another prank which I witnessed, and to this day will as far as I'm concerned go down as one of the best, was when the resident sparky was conducting some work in the koala exhibit. A keeper, who was looking on, made a peacock calling impersonation, so good that it scared the unsuspecting worker. When coming back several days later a real peacock jumped up onto the fence behind the sparky and began to call, the sparky stood up and announced that he wasn't going to be fooled this time, much to the disappointed look on the real peacock sitting on the fence behind him.

During rather hot weather we would always end up in or creating a water fight, visiting other departments while they were having their break in a van full of buckets of water, sometimes ice cold, this would result in having the same carried out on us.

During a hot spell we decided to drench a senior member of staff, the Head of Keeping, and after having several buckets of water in the fridge overnight for such a purpose we called her on the radio requesting her presence in the Slaughterhouse or should I say the CDPC. Upon arrival she gladly handed her radio to a staff member before entering the building, even though the person requesting her radio already had one. Upon reaching the back area of the building she was greeted by me and several others resulting in an instant dowsing of cold water. Several days later we wanted her to come to the same building, with no evil intentions mind, upon which we received a flat no for an answer.

Last but not least the one major prank I played on fellow carnivore keepers, that we often laugh about when recalling. While attending to the Syrian Bears I noticed a fresh pile of soil that had been deposited directly behind their off-limit area. I decided to acquire the loan of a stuffed skunk from the nearby Education Department, which I placed at the base of the fresh mound with some soil pushed behind it, to give the impression that it was in the process of digging a hole. When one of my fellow colleagues came past I brought it to his attention, thinking that he would appreciate the effort that I had gone to. The reaction from him was that he believed that it was a real live skunk, and we got into a discussion as to how to catch it. I informed him that I had just read a book the night before on how to catch one. To his horror I ran at it and picked it up revealing that indeed it was stuffed. After much cursing from my unintended victim we replanted it back into place only to catch another unsuspecting victim.

However there was indeed a price to pay and for weeks I was very concerned as to when the repercussion would fall on me. Several weeks later with the crew on the way to the Lion Park to do some much-needed work, I was asked to feed the bears and let them out, and then to meet them at the Lion Park. Counting that the three bears were safely secured within the off-limit area, I picked up their food to distribute into their display. As I opened the exhibit door there before me was our resident stuffed Polar Bear propped up on its hind legs. I stood mortified and upon closing the door fell to the ground in total disbelief, only to hear roaring laughter coming from the front of the exhibit where my bent-on-revenge fellow colleagues stood. One of them came running around to where I was wondering if I had had a heart attack. I at least could walk around from then on without looking over my shoulder.

The said Polar Bear raised its ugly head again when it was placed in the Operations Manager's office. The end result being that upon returning from her weekend off, she received a shock to her system as I had. The said polar bear I believe now resides in the Melbourne Museum on full public display where it can no longer be used for pranks.

CHAPTER 15

At One with the Public

We always remained aware that almost inevitably there would be comments made to us by the general public as we went about our business in enclosures, and most of the time we would prefer to ignore them. They were the usual "Oh what type of animal is that?" Directed at the keeper inside the exhibit, or some other comment that we would have heard numerous times before. The best way was to not give anyone the satisfaction of becoming annoyed or concerned, in any way shape or form, however it was sometimes just too much of a temptation from time to time to allow a smart sharp reply to part from our lips.

While cleaning a kangaroo display a keeper was on the receiving end of a barrage of rude comments from a visitor who was attempting to impress his girlfriend. The keeper in question made no effort to react to him, but in an act of sheer arrogance began to look at his girlfriend with a mischievous smile on his face resulting in the girlfriend being ushered away by her rather annoyed boyfriend.

While a colleague assisted me in carrying one of our large male giant tortoises into its heated house late one winters evening, a member of the public enquired as we carried it "how heavy was it?" only to get a reply of "F###ing real heavy lady".

A seal keeper while doing a public talk and being hassled by one of the female seals announced, "Now you know why they call female seals COWS!"

Some visitors would be horrified and complain that the zoo allowed animals to copulate while on display.

While some of our Japanese tourists would ask where the 'Qantases' were, as the Qantas ads in Japan featured Koalas, with the assumption that that was what they were called.

While feeding penguins during the Easter holidays I was asked by a member of the public if I was going to feed them Easter Eggs? "No, I replied but as it is good Friday I will feed them fish today."

Another time while being on the receiving end of a severe barrage of insults,

I informed the said insulters that I get paid to be here while they paid to be here, which resulted in a huge round of applause.

So as you can well imagine it's always wise to say or do nothing unless of course the opportunity arises that you can rise above them, with a resounding reply.

Some visitors would approach you to take a group photo, and we were always willing to comply. One particular gentleman, if you could call him that, approached me on a very busy day to perform such a request. The area they had chosen for the group photograph was on the main drive, seriously obstructing the passing crowds. I suggested an area just off to the side that would provide them with a flower garden background. The response that I got to this sensible suggestion was greeted with some anger, bordering on verbal abuse. I then considered whether to refuse this request and just walk away. As quick as a flash I came up with another alternative, and as they gathered in the inappropriate spot I took several photos and in handing back the camera got no word of thanks from them taking up my time to provide such an additional service. Digital cameras were not in existence at the time and I had great satisfaction in knowing that when they did get this particular roll of film processed the photos that I took would be just of their feet.

While leaning over the fence of the otter enclosure a woman somehow dropped part of her false teeth, which happened to fall into a pile of otter faeces. Now otter deposits are without doubt one of the vilest sort of deposits that one can encounter. Even for keepers, as it consists of remnants of fish and yabbies, which after passing through an otter not only stinks but looks disgusting. After her son had reported the incident to one of the keeping staff, as the woman who had lost her dentures could not speak English, the said dentures were retrieved from the pile of excrement. The keeper informed the son that the dentures needed to be washed several times and then soaked in a sterilisation solution even before considering putting them back into her mouth. Upon telling his mother this important information, she promptly placed them back in her mouth, much to the horror of the informant. So much for otter mouth wash and halitosis!

A family was threatened by a knife-wielding man after they told him off for teasing some birds. After receiving the complaint the police were called, only to apprehend the assailant and his friends at the railway station at the back entrance of the zoo. A knife was found in the station's rubbish bin, and by the way the police handled the situation it was obvious that the man was known to them.

An ice-cream van would always be parked outside the zoo, in a designated area that he could park his truck, along with all the appropriate permits. Business was always brisk over the years for him, and he would always greet his customers with a friendly smile. Being in a prime position visitors to the zoo would purchase ice-creams from him as they came or went. Trade was brisk and he would often engage in conversation with zoo staff, offering them discount ice creams, which was always appreciated.

After catching a schoolboy red-handed throwing stones at the giraffes, and after his numerous efforts to deny such a charge, his teacher was called to meet with us. After some time of denial he eventually admitted to his actions. The teacher insisted that he apologise to me, which he did, then added that I should be more observant in my job to prevent this type of behaviour. I replied suggesting that I had done just that by catching him out, and maybe he should be evicted from the zoo. He was escorted away with the teacher firmly holding his arm, informing him that he would be spending the remainder of the day waiting in the bus. A case of justice served.

Llamas have a putrid disgusting habit or behaviour of being able to regurgitate food from their stomachs and spit it all over you. One such Llama took a complete disliking towards keeping staff and would take every opportunity to cover a keeper with his vile stomach treats. Several keepers while passing the Llamas' paddock made loud hissing noises at it as they were at a safe distance. The Llama then expelled its stomach contents over a woman who was admiring the animal at the fence. She thought that she was the chosen one and that the Llama had paid her a compliment, the keepers assisted her with a free zoo tee shirt to take home as a souvenir.

Another episode involving this delightful animal was a keeper who while poking his tongue out at a llama as it was attempting to spit on him over an off-limit fence, unfortunately slipped on the wet ground only to find himself face up at the mercy of the llama and received a well-deserved vile green pasting over his face.

An old zoo story tells the story of a well-dressed woman in her summer array, who asked that a nearby keeper to encourage the llama to spit. "No, you wouldn't Madam" came the reply and informed her of the unpleasantness of the act. After the keeper moved on to attend to his other duties she provoked the animal with her dainty white parasol. And while the llama tolerated such a behaviour for a while, his powers in the end were tested, with the llama rising to the occasion and covering the tormentor with a vile smelling green semi liquid. So there was a woman who would never in the future request such an action from a llama.

Another story relevant to this subject was a woman who asked a gardener "Do you know when the lions are fed?" He informed her that he did and went about his work. Thinking that he did not hear her correctly, she asked the question again, only to get the same reply. Then she asked him if he had heard what she had said? "I did" came the reply. Calling him impertinent he asked why? "I asked you if you knew when the lions are fed," he then informed her that he did know and that she did not ask him what time they were to be fed.

Some visitors were just plain rude and on one occasion a son of a VIP was given permission to be allowed in the Red Panda enclosure, under my supervision. Meanwhile his mother stood outside the enclosure talking rather loudly on her phone, at times getting so loud her son could not hear what I was saying. As she kept up this annoying behaviour I politely asked her if she could move away elsewhere as I'm sure the Red Panda was becoming rather apprehensive. She looked at me as if I had slapped her around the face and made some indication that she found me impertinent and rude. I informed her that she was the rude one, upon which she instructed her son to come out of the enclosure and walked away dragging her disappointed son behind her. Several days later another request was made from her, and it was declined. One would have thought that she could have taken time out the first time to enjoy the experience.

One visitor rushed up to me grunting "tigers, tigers". Knowing that he wished to be directed to them I indicated to him that yes we did have tigers. He looked at me with an angry face and got quite close to me, and at one stage I thought he was going to strike me. I asked him politely to move away and once again he yelled "tiger." His wife standing just to the side walked up to him and quietly in another language whispered into his ear. He paused, moved slightly away from me and in a much more civil tone asked me if he could direct me to the tiger enclosure, which I did.

A young schoolgirl was suspiciously approached by a male person at the pygmy hippo viewing windows, and we were quick to get that adult in the hands of the police. No harm was done to the student, but the male involved was arrested by the police.

While conducting a behind the scenes experience, which gave the visitors an opportunity to feed a tiger through a feeding area in the off-limit section, one woman informed me, as many did, that tigers were her favourite animal and that she had many pet domestic cats at home. I nodded my head in acknowledgement of her passion for tigers, upon which she made the statement "I wonder what they taste like?" That I could not tell her, and I wonder to this day if she maybe has eaten one of her cats in her endeavour to find out, hopefully not.

While waiting in a queue on the way to work at a petrol station the person in front of me turned and noticed my zoo uniform, asking me if I worked at the zoo, upon which I looked down at my zoo badge and told him, "Well I must according to what I'm wearing".

One winter's evening as I was ushering visitors from the Reptile House I came across the last of the visitors, a group of bikies, all in their colours and all of them huge in size and muscular. They were in front of the crocodile exhibit and as I approached them I had visions of this being my final minutes on the face of the earth. However as they all turned towards me they made kind, polite comments on their experience within the facility and left without any issues at all.

One thing we found difficult to tolerate were 'window tappers,' who were under the impression that by carrying out such an act they could get the animal in the exhibit to move or respond in some way. It was a big Public Holiday crowd and the act of window tapping on the reptile house windows that we could hear from the off-limit area was in full swing and getting worse. It got so bad that we decided to venture out into the public gallery to curb the behaviour in some way. It took some time to track down the culprits, a group of men with their children in tow, seeing if one can get as many reptiles to move as if it was some kind of competition. I followed them just to confirm that it was them, and once I had established this I approached them, as it was wall-to-wall people they had the excuse to pretend that they could not hear us, as they are not too far from the exit we waited for them outside. When they appeared we took them aside to explain that their actions were not appreciated. One took it that we were hassling them when I said that that's exactly what they had been doing to the residents of the Reptile House. I then informed them that they could easily be escorted out of the zoo, if this was their attitude. Next thing out of nowhere came the wives shouting at them for walking too fast in front of them and knocking on the windows. Justice had been done, thanks to the wives' club.

Above: My first visit to the zoo with a ride on the carousel still in operation today.

Right: My favourite childhood pastime with Shingleback Lizards and Cunningham Skinks.

Below: One of the zoo's resident Black Headed Pythons.

PHOTO COURTESY OF ROBERT BAIRD / HERALD SUN

Above: 'Iggy' the Rhinocerous Iguana who would often be given the opportunity to explore the reptile off-limit areas.

Opposite above: with one of our three Sumatran tigers born at Melbourne Zoo.

Opposite below: A visit to Melbourne Zoo from Dad.

PHOTO COURTESY OF MARK SMITH, HERALD SUN

Above: A hand raised ring tailed possum in the Education Keeping Department called 'Dead end', due to missing the end of her tail.

Below: A session with our female orangutan Kiani, she lived to 45 years of age, the oldest orangutan in Melbourne Zoo.

Precious moments with Mzuri, the first surviving gorilla in the world conceived by artificial insemination.

PHOTO COURTESY
MARK SMITH /
HERALD SUN

Opposite: Female Sumatran Tiger, Indra.
Above: Kruger, one of our male Lions waiting to be fed.
Below: A curious Snow Leopard.

Above: A getting to know you session with a male Giraffe calf born at Melbourne Zoo.
Opposite: A final check of Jandamarra prior to his road trip to Werribee Open Range Zoo. PHOTO COURTESY OF JAY TOWN / HERALD SUN

MELB

Above: One on one with a male Rothschild Giraffe.
Opposite above: A female Lioness at Monbulk Reptile and Fauna Reserve.
Opposite below: Lois the Leopard Cat.

Opposite: Holding one of the Lion cubs born at Monbulk Reptile and Fauna Reserve.
Above: Feeding time for the Lions at Melbourne Zoo.
Below: Feeding one of the Red Pandas.

PHOTO COURTESY OF BEN SWINNERTON / HERALD SUN

Above: Lions at Bacchus Marsh Lion Park.

Opposite. A swim session with the Seals at Melbourne Zoo.

PHOTO COURTESY OF JAY TOWN / HERALD SUN

My passion for painting the animals I've worked with. A Sumatran tiger, Hamadryas Baboon and Mandrill Baboon.

FRONT COVER PHOTO COURTESY JAY TOWN HERALD SUN

CHAPTER 16

On the Wrong Side of the Fence

There was always someone who thought that it would be a good idea to find a way to be at one with one of the animals by getting in with them, without considering the consequences of their actions. There have been numerous incidents over the years where this has happened, and most of the time the intruders have been fortunate to have survived.

A teacher arrived at the back gate of the zoo to notice a naked man on one of the nearby Gibbon Islands, the island in fact that housed one of the most aggressive primates. Upon arriving in the office and reporting the incident this was greeted with much laughter for it was April Fool's Day. And no one was going to fall for that. So with the Education crew in tow with one of the animal curators it didn't take long to see that it was no joke. The naked individual was by this time hanging out his washing on a makeshift line and had a fire going to cook his breakfast. With the gibbon with a bad reputation, sitting high in one of the trees looking down at the intruder, who remained unscathed until he was removed. The incident made front page in all the major papers.

While watching the lions a visitor incurred a finger injury, by one of the resident lions. As the injury resulted in some or most of her finger being severed, it was investigated, and the injured visitor after much questioning changed her story from leaning well over the safety barrier to pick some flowers which were never there, to attempting to touch a lion as it walked passed. She did not expect the animal to react so quickly.

In another case a young student jumped over the safety fence of the Big Cat Complex and subsequently got too close to the wire. The Persian Leopard managed to remove the sleeve of his jacket, leaving him with some nasty wounds to his hand and arm. To this day I am still bewildered that he escaped more serious injuries than what he received from the encounter.

During a busy weekend someone was observed over the main safety fence at the Elephant Display and being Head Animal Person for that day I had to attend the incident where a man was being spoken to by staff. As luck would have it, he experienced a moment of common sense to back away from one of the fences where one of the elephants was attempting to grab one of his legs to drag him under the barrier. It was obvious after talking to him for some time with the police, that he believed he had the right to carry out such an act of sheer stupidity. The police took no action against him, and I recommended that he stay away from the zoo as a way of self-preservation.

Late one evening a man jumped into the lion enclosure, after hiding in bushes after closing time to test out his Karate skills. The resident curator and his wife heard the lions carrying on, and assumed that they were fighting, not much one can do when that occurs. They were in fact tearing apart the intruder with only a torso found being carried across the exhibit in the morning and discovered by a passing keeper. Several body parts were found several days later, and the following weekend you could not get anywhere near the Lion Park due to the crowds. Who said the days of the Colosseum are over?

Another individual jumped in with the lions after scaling the fence, and was fortunate to exit alive, as we managed to get him into the off-limit caged area before he was attacked. He attempted it again sometime later and got away with it again. Several years later while the lions were in their off-limit areas, he once again managed to scale the fence and ended up in with the lions when they were let out into the viewing area. Once again he managed to get away with it unscathed, much to our amazement. Upon being informed that such an act was not only very dangerous but stressful to the occupants he apologised and never attempted the act again. His photo was displayed in the admission office so he could be identified and turned away if he attempted to visit the zoo again.

One hot day a young visitor decided to impress his girlfriend by jumping into the Bison Enclosure, taking his t-shirt off to play matador with the bison. Fortunately for him the female was on display, as if it had been the male, it would have been a totally different story. He received some chest injuries as a result of having to be dragged out of the moat. Even after this he could not totally comprehend the results of his action, not understanding why he was escorted from the property. Maybe a demonstration of the result and impact of a bison attack would have given him a clearer message, but then again maybe not.

Peccaries are species of South American pigs with a huge set of extremely sharp teeth. We had some seven in our collection. One day a drunken visitor sat himself down on a rock in the centre of the display and proceeded to roll himself a cigarette. As the Peccaries surrounded him, bristling with sheer aggression, he just went about smoking and drinking and pondering his next move. While we were locking up the pigs, enticing them into their dens with food, the intruder left, surprised at all the panic going on around him.

One caring parent was observed placing his 3-year-old daughter over the safety fence at Baboons with a banana in her hand, only to punish her when we approached him, when he should have been the one punished.

A family of six decided to make their way through the garden bed at the back of the new lion enclosure, and scaled one of the safety fences, placing them in direct contact with the lions via the main back fence. Fortunately I had observed the act from a distance, and quickly proceeded to shout out to them, and have them removed not only from their dangerous position but from the premises altogether. They reluctantly left after failing to have their admission fee refunded and informing me that they believed that they had done nothing wrong.

One of the most consistently popular behaviours by the public was to jump into the giant tortoises enclosure and photograph each other sitting on the tortoises.

One last episode, that was on the right side of the fence, but worth telling was the day my son came in with his school excursion and I conducted a behind the scenes lion feed for them to witness. This involved getting all nine lions into individual feeding dens with a wire front. Once all the lions were in and secure I proceeded to feed the hungry occupants. Once finished I turned my back on the class while informing them that I was going to let the lions out. I heard some scurrying and turned to see the school group all crowded against the opposite wall thinking that I was for some reason going to let the lions out of their enclosure, needless to say that the only child left standing unperturbed was my son who had witnessed the lion feeding several times before.

Stories have been told when visitors would throw bags full of dirt and stones into the Hippos Enclosure, hoping to lob the object into their mouths. Hippos have died after consuming tennis balls thrown in with them.

Some visitors would just step over a barrier or walk through a gate undetected, giving them the opportunity to look or snoop around. Some were so casual about it that they were at times mistaken for a contractor. When questioned they would attempt to come up with some pathetic excuse, and then they would be quickly escorted back to the public area.

These are just a few examples of many, where the public believe they have a right for a free and last close encounter.

CHAPTER 17

Saying Our Goodbyes

Everyone knows how sad and devastating it is when a pet passes away, whether it's from illness or old age, and it's equally as devastating for keepers, having developed close bonds with zoo inhabitants, sometimes caring for them for many years. There have been numerous times when some of our charges have passed away, and there has been many a time after such a loss when I have taken myself off for a quiet walk, as other keepers have either around the zoo grounds, or in an off-limit area to grieve and remember how honoured we have been to have had the animal in our care. There have been some significant losses. The loss of our Black Jaguar, Maya, hit me very hard indeed, as he was a perfect example of wisdom, strength, and beauty that to this day I miss so much. Mukulu the Giraffe, Trish the Ocelot were other ones as well as the Black Leopards and of course Rigo, the silverback Gorilla, having been there when he died. The lions from the original Lion Park have all passed away but will never pass away in my mind and the memories of them still remain.

Even now from time to time we receive the news of the passing of one of the animals that we have worked with and cared for, stirring up precious memories of times we have spent with them and how honoured we are to have played a part in their lives. I still have numerous images of them pasted away in a photo book, in fact my wife presented me with a photo book full of photos of me and many of the animals I have described not long after I had left the zoo.

CHAPTER 18

Off-limits

Melbourne Zoo's Food Store was and still is the life blood of the zoo. It's the supermarket of the zoo, and up until 1973 it was operated by just one person. All that changed after a review of the animals' diets, and an extra person was put on. The Food Store staff would be able to purchase from the Footscray market a week's supply of fruit and vegetables off the back of trucks that would be backed up, side-by-side where farmers sell their produce. From the $385 food store budget some $130 of this would purchase all the fruit and veggies for the zoo for a whole week. The meat for the carnivores was picked up from a slaughterhouse in Maffra, some 230 km away, with the staff bringing back some four-odd tonnes of meat in two trucks, arriving back at the zoo well after dark. They would then have to store it all in the Carnivore Department's freezer. Chickens, cartons of eggs, and processed minced meat were also on the menu. A large table was set up in the centre of the food store where numerous trays were positioned containing a huge range of food where keepers prepared food from various departments. Silos containing food pellets or grains that were loaded from the outside via shutes. The mezzanine floor was filled with bags of other food items and other items used from day to day. All this to feed a large collection of animals. Today there is just the one store person who visits the Victoria Market once a week to bring back fruit and vegetables, even whole watermelons that have not sold, yet are of good quality, most or all of it being free of charge, saving the zoo thousands of dollars a year. Unsold bread from the day before collected from the nearby bakery, including rolls, crumpets etc. Some of these items were used to feed the elephants and other animals, as well as some of it ending up in zoo staff rooms to be toasted for morning tea or lunch. Another item that was delivered to the food store was Madeira cake that came in large slabs intended for the Bird Department. From time-to-time staff would take some for their own departments, often leaving the Bird Department short, only to have most or some of it to reappear when the call went out on the radio for it to be returned. Huge deliveries of lucerne, hay and straw would be delivered at the hay sheds, and keeping staff would assist in offloading several trucks at a time. A long time before I started the food store had a resident cat called Moog. It didn't roam far at all and could be often found asleep in some area of the store. The Curator of Birds and Reptiles lived in a small house directly opposite the Food store, and on most or every second evening could be seen walking back across from the zoo supermarket with a basketful of goodies for his tea. The Food store still stands today as it has for many years.

The Humpy

The Humpy, as it was affectionately known, was in fact the Native Mammal office. Most departments had their own offices and staff rooms at the time it was converted from a storage tool shed. It deserves a mention as it was the major meeting place for most of the keeping staff at the zoo, before work and for morning and afternoon teas. There was also outdoor furniture that was used when it wasn't raining. There were a number of rules set down by the Keeper in charge due to the high visitation rate. It was a place where you could polish your work boots, make a coffee or tea, or just sit, chatting and catching up with all the local zoo news. It was one warm summer's day that I was sitting close to one of the outer walls when I heard a loud humming, and after having the humming noise confirmed by others it turned out to be a huge European Wasp nest. Today the Humpy exists no more, consumed by time, and replaced by a new office that somehow just doesn't feel the same.

Living in the Zoo

At the time I was there some staff members resided on the premises. One staff member built a boat in the back of his residence that had to be craned out when he left. Today I believe that no staff members live within the walls of the zoo. There are several houses still in existence, some are used as offices or storage areas. They remain as part of the zoo's history. Many years ago one of the major television stations ran a show about a family living in the zoo, keepers were at times given the opportunity to be involved. I was in the Reptile House and the film crew came down to film some scenes, one where I am in the background opening a door for one of the actors. As I was standing watching them film, the Director yelled out "cut," only to look in my direction with a questioning look on his face as to ask why I was not in my designated place.

At the end of filming the whole crew made themselves available to do some comedy skits for a Golden Nugget Award Night.

CHAPTER 19

Read All About It, the Public Relations Machine

We often found ourselves doing our bit for PR promoting the zoo, such as the birth of a giraffe, or television shows such as *Talk to the Animals*. It could be rather time-consuming, but everyone got the chance for their five minutes of fame, some more than others. Some presenters would contact you by phone the day before and get as much information as they could from you about the topic, and then on the day would come across as if they themselves were a wealth of information on the subject, and you were a complete idiot with them knowing more about the subject than you.

My very first exposure being involved with the zoo public relations was when I received a phone call from the *Truth* newspaper while working on reptiles. Now the *Truth* newspaper was a Melbourne tabloid. It was a sensational weekly paper with stories involving scandals, court reports, and images of semi-naked women. I assumed that the zoo's PR Department had transferred them to the Reptile House to interview me. The subject which they wished to discuss was the use of cobra blood and bile being claimed to be the world's best aphrodisiac. I innocently gave my opinions on the subject. The following week's issue of *Truth* had an article on page three titled 'Snake potion puts bite on sex,' quoting what I and other people in the field had commented on the subject. To make matters spicier, the article was published under a photo of a topless woman. I was within a short period of time contacted by the zoo's PR department with a please explain? Another learning curve in my career. And I can honestly say even to this day that I appeared in the *Truth* newspaper under a semi-naked woman!

The Age newspaper decided to run a feature in their Sunday Life supplement, and the PR department chose me to do it. This involved being followed around by a journalist for most of the day as I carried out my daily tasks, as well as being interviewed and asked a myriad of questions. I was surprised at the quality of the resulting article achieved, giving the public a view of what a keepers daily workday is really like.

Stihl Power tools had donated a hedge trimmer and several other items to the zoo, in exchange for obtaining a photograph of the zoo's gardeners using it. This was to be used for a promotional pamphlet. The gardener who was selected to do it didn't turn up, and as I was walking nearby I was nabbed by the other gardeners and photographed using the trimmer. Little did they know that hedge trimmers are not in a zookeeper's arsenal. They sent me a full promotional photo which I still, or should I say stihl! have to this day!

Another newspaper ran an article on dangerous jobs, which included a high-rise window cleaner, and me as a Lion Tamer, under the heading 'Danger is my Business.' There was a photo of me with one of the tigers, minus the chair and whips.

The ABC ran a series on the operation of the three zoo properties called *Zoo's Company*, with a behind the scenes look at what keepers face every day in their working lives. It covered many areas and followed various departments from primates to carnivores, catch ups and other events.

Another program was put together by another television station and involved filming Australian Pythons, where they had one set up in an enclosure with a glass front to aid uninterrupted filming. I assisted with the set up but over time became rather concerned as to the way in which they wanted to go about it. As I was responsible for the welfare of the reptile, I pulled the python from the project as the conditions were not meeting the standards that I had asked for. I wasn't Mr Popularity with the film crew, but I was working in the best interests of the python, and that after all was the most important thing.

A paper ran another article on myself and several other keepers, it was titled 'The Wild Bunch,' and had a typing error claiming that one of my favourite snakes was the Emerald Tree Boa, but in the article it was an 'Emil Tree Boa'. Which was a lie as I've never worked with 'Emil Tree Boas' and didn't know they even existed.

Numerous other articles appeared with yours truly in it when it came down to vaccinating animals or a new baby born. It was all part of the PR machine.

CHAPTER 20

Weather or Not

We would work in all types of weather conditions, from the chill of winter where we would crack open the icy surface of animal water bowls, to enduring days of constant rain for days on end. Our Driza-Bone full length raincoats and hats would become heavy as they never quite got the opportunity to dry out from the day to day use. It was during heat spells that we would often arrive home totally spent. These occasions were the time that we had to pay close attention to our charges offering them food in ice blocks and keeping the sprinklers on, as well as giving them access to their dens and off-limit yards, putting out signs to what members of the public were still around to advise them that the animal they might want to see has access and may not be on display. We would always look after ourselves as well with cold or hot drinks. Long periods of rain and cold or heat would wear us down and we would get the opportunity to stay indoors to carry out some research or paperwork. It was never a problem when working with the seals during the summer months and even during winter when we could wear wetsuits to protect us from the elements. It was all part of the job weather we liked it or not!

CHAPTER 21

Zoo Twilights and Corporate Nights

The Zoo Twilight series had humble beginnings during summer, with a jazz band playing on the small bandstand near the Reptile House. Visitors could come after hours to enjoy the sights and sounds of the zoo, while enjoying some food and wine. The implementation of Twilights was of course to increase the amount of income for the zoo. However this also presented several important issues as to the impact that this would have on the animals. They were always comfortable in a routine, and this meant that they would be given access, and in some cases as with the Gorillas, fed later than usual. There was also the issue of how much extra the staff were to be paid. The union became involved and after much deliberation an agreement was met. The lawn area would soon be covered with picnic blankets and people enjoying a glass of wine and food. Eventually over the years a large stage was constructed to replace the bandstand which had become inadequate for the event. The first act on the stage was the *ABBA* cover group *BABA*, the crowd got so large the gates were closed, as the zoo could not accommodate more visitors safely. The cover group was invited back again for a repeat performance which resulted in more full capacity crowds. Over the years jazz bands were replaced with the likes of celebrities such as Paul Kelly, Daryl Braithwaite, Leo Sayer, just to name a few. With a much larger better equipped sound stage, the event became very popular, and soon huge crowds would gather at the gates eager to get in and secure themselves a prime spot near the stage. These nights would run at first four days a week from Thursday to Sunday evenings.

Staying back after a full day's work was tiring, and at times demanding. We not only had to make sure that the animals were secured, but make sure that all of the Twilight crowd were on the lawn area at a certain time, before the start of the show. By the end of the show the visitors, with full bellies and at times a little on the inebriated side, would show little or no interest as we did in heading for home, so we'd go around to groups and parties of people not only asking them if they had enjoyed themselves, which we knew they had, but also to politely get them to move on to the exit gates, without coming across as party poopers. Most would comply but there was always a group that thought that the evening included overtime. It got at times rather draining to have to approach them several times before they got the message that they needed to leave. Some would make a comment back to you which you would just smile through clenched teeth and tell them that you were glad they had a great time. While what you really wanted to tell them was that you had been at the zoo since 7am that morning while they were still asleep in bed and had put in a solid day's work and the current time would tell them if they did the maths that you had been at work for just on 14 hours and that you really just wanted them to go home so you could do the same.

Following groups out to the main front or back gates was at times slow and arduous, with some visitors wanting to turn down a pathway in order to explore other areas of the zoo at night.

One couple walking a considerable distance ahead of me suddenly ducked into some thick bushes, with the intention of playing silly games with me or to part take in some sexual activity, like "Let's get hot and dirty at the zoo". It turned out to be the latter, and by the time I got to the bushes, and above the heavy breathing and rustling, I announced that the zoo was closed, and that I would appreciate them making their way to the exit. After several moments of getting themselves looking half decent they emerged, somewhat disappointed at having their sexual intentions gatecrashes.

On another evening while walking the grounds with the Operations Manager, we got a radio call that a visitor was defecating in a nearby garden bed. Upon our arrival the reported deed had been carried out, and the perpetrator was just exiting the garden where she had made her deposit. After questioning her we escorted her to the back gate where we received a barrage of vile verbal abuse, for what? Not cleaning up after her! She later returned as we were securing the back gates only to ask if she could be allowed access to the grounds so she could walk up to the main entrance to meet a friend. Flatly refusing to accommodate her, we were once again hit with a barrage of foul language, only for her sister who was nearby to give us an added mouthful.

Nearby the zoo at Yarra Bend Park, a Grey-headed Flying Fox colony exists. As they are nocturnal, thousands would be seen flying over the zoo at the end of Twilights, on the nightly search for food. One woman while walking with me to the front entrance at the end of a Twilight night, was amazed at the number of birds flying over, only to be informed that they were fruit bats. She quickly informed me that bats only exist in vampire movies, and she would appreciate me not telling such stories as it was upsetting her daughter walking alongside her. A clear case of the truth hurts.

Some visitors would take their behaviour to the very limit. One such incident during Twilights was the distribution of photos of a young woman sitting on the toilet, being thrown into the Gorilla enclosure. When reported the man responsible was approached, after we waited for him to exit one of our toilets and questioned, he casually came up with some excuse for his behaviour. Meanwhile the police who had been called arrived, and he was taken into custody. He was known to the police, and we took the necessary action to ensure that a photo of him would be posted up at admissions to ensure he would never be allowed into the zoo again, much the same as our "Let's get in with the lions" visitor.

One afternoon a storm raged through the zoo grounds, bringing down branches and dumping torrents of rain with it. The officer in charge of Twilights for that evening chose to cancel the event, unaware that a huge crowd had already turned up, and had become angry that what they had come to see was not going to happen. It was decided from then on that whatever the weather the show would go on. On the evening of the very next Twilight Night heavy rain fell, drenching the zoo's Twilight Lawn area, which resulted in a very small crowd, being accommodated in the Zoo's Bistro, with the booked band playing for a much smaller crowed than they ever anticipated. Sometimes you just can't win.

The last Twilight episode well worth mentioning involved a couple who had had a rather loud verbal altercation with one another, with the woman, who had an infant in a pusher, demanding the car keys from her partner. The police were called to sort them out as we would never intervene in such domestic disputes. After notes and statements were made the couple made up and were escorted from the grounds. On reaching their car, the couple jumped into the back seat to have make up sex while their infant sat outside the car enjoying the views of the carpark from his pusher. Perfect example of 'Happy Families'.

During the summer period the zoo also provided Corporate Nights for major companies that would hire out the zoo for several hours, at great expense. Tables would be set up at strategic points around the zoo so they could be waited upon by catering staff to partake in a selection of expensive wines, hors d'oeuvres, canapés etc. and have a keeper positioned within those areas to give talks. There were usually three or four groups that would come through at set times. My first group consisted of around 20 people with the majority of them on their mobile phones, making personal or business calls, all talking loudly over one another and me as I attempted to give my presentation. By the third group I just gave up. I stood drooling as they drank, ate and talked on their mobiles. The last group of the evening was no different, I felt if they were interested enough which apparently they were not, they would approach me with a query or question. One woman eventually did, asking me where the nearest toilets were! I'm so glad that I could be of assistance that evening.

CHAPTER 22

Celebrities and Tantrums

We were often called upon to entertain or assist with some PR. One such TV celebrity, who had a weekly lifestyle show on television, came to the zoo several times, and on one occasion wanted to film a segment in front of the Otter Display. I met him and his film crew at the service gate and escorted him to the selected location. As the sound and camera men were setting up he sat quietly nearby chain smoking, until the time arrived for him to do his presentation. The sound man at the time was having difficulties with his equipment and the filming had to stop several times. This apparently was too much for the presenter, and he flew into an abusive meltdown of pure rage and obscenities. I had to remind him of the presence of some school children watching the proceeding nearby, and teachers who were looking on, and that he needed to curb his vile language. After the sound man corrected the issue everything ran smoothly and on schedule again. They soon departed without a word of thanks, except for the film crew who now knew that I knew what they had to put up with.

Another celebrity wanted to film staff catching up Meerkats for their vaccinations. The front of the display was glass so they could film through it without any obstacles. However the celebrity in question wanted to film the process from inside the display, which I pointed out to him would create too many obstacles for the Meerkats to run into and would impede the catch up procedure. This did not however seem to be a major concern to him, and I made it clear that the only way he was going to get the footage was from outside the display. I thought that at one stage he was going to look for a staff member who could override my decision, however everything went to plan, and they got excellent footage of a perfect example of capture and restraint of the thirteen Meerkats. On escorting him back to his vehicle it was obvious that to him I no longer existed, which made me aware that what viewers see on their television screens, does not always tell the whole story.

I was called up to the Tiger Enclosure by public relations to supervise what I thought was to be a promotional item on tigers. When I arrived I was confronted by a film crew all dressed up in safari suits and imitation rifles. They wanted to do an act for a show, whereby I informed them in no uncertain terms that it was not in any way appropriate to film such a thing in a zoo and not something that was going to happen. They looked at me with disappointed expressions on their faces and in the end left without anything on film. Maybe going somewhere else, I didn't care so long as it was not at the zoo. I believe that someone had arranged this without the approval of the Public Relations Department.

On a good note we had a famous American actress and her husband visit to get a firsthand behind the scenes look at some young lion cubs. They were so impressed with the experience, that they issued the zoo with a cheque for $10,000. Looking back at the generous offer I should have changed my name to Mr Melbourne Zoo.

Many years before, the Native Mammal Department got involved with a visit from Jimmy Stewart, an American actor who appeared in many films such as *Rear Window*, *Vertigo*, and *It's A Wonderful Life,* just to name a few. He was well into his eighties at the time and not in the best of moods on that particular day, refusing to hold a koala when it was offered to him. The segment was aired on television that night which didn't do much for Mr Stewart's profile.

One of the most pleasant public relations experiences I had was with a well-known news presenter who would often visit the zoo to do some great presentations for the television viewing public. At this time I was with him at the Tiger Enclosure where he was attempting to remember the names of all the tigers, which he kept forgetting and constantly messing up his lines, which resulted in us falling about with laughter. He eventually got it right after several takes.

On being late for lunch I was eager to sit down and relax, and just as I was nearing the Carnivore Staff Room I was contacted on the radio to return to the front of the Tiger Enclosure. It was there that I was greeted by two AFL football greats, and I was more than willing to get the tigers to come down to the front of their enclosure, for them to get a better look at them. I spent the best part of several hours showing them around and also giving them a lion feed. A day that I will always remember, even though it cost me a lunch break.

At times we would not leave the zoo until around 10.30pm only to know that we would be back the following day to do it all over again. With Twilights and the roster we worked, this presented us with very long days working some twelve days straight, and with Twilights in the mix we were always glad to drive home knowing that we had some days off to relax and spend with the family.

CHAPTER 23

Christmas and I Do at the Zoo

Every year a huge Christmas dinner was put on by management and it would be followed by some staff being able to take a half a day off on full pay to give them a chance to partake in some Christmas shopping. With other staff members who were to stay behind to follow suit the next day. The Freeman family who owned and operated the Fun Fair would open the gates for free rides, ice-cream and fairy floss for all the keepers' children, with the adults bringing eskies full of roast chicken and champagne, with of course a staff member making their appearance as Santa. The Fun Fair opened in 1952, the year I was born, and closed down in 1997 after 45 years. The Freemans who operated the Fun Fair were always friendly and generous to towards us. Christmas Day at the zoo, believe it or not, was always popular, with one family that would come every year and set up trestle tables for their huge family and enjoy the surrounds of the zoo. Other members of the public who didn't celebrate Christmas also made a day of it at the zoo. For staff rostered on they would organise in advance what everyone would bring, roast pork, chicken, mince tarts, rum balls, a feast with all the trimmings. Then at lunch time would meet up in the Education Centre to enjoy the huge Christmas banquet. Departments would work in advance to allow rostered-on staff to just perform the very basic duties and be able to take an extended lunch break, some being able to go home earlier to enjoy what was left of the day with their families. Keepers who had children would often swap days and have Christmas Day off and work New Year's Day. It was always a busy time but one that we somehow enjoyed working.

One year we decided to put on our own production of the *Rocky Horror Show*, with yours truly playing the part of Riff Raff. This one and only performance was held in one of the huge sheds at Werribee Open Range Zoo. Rehearsals were carried out in secret, usually after work, with the odd one now and then at lunch times. I would go about my work rehearsing my lines every chance I got, at times getting strange looks from anyone in earshot. As the date got closer we had a full dress-rehearsal to ensure that we had it all down pat. As we had the soundtrack, we all mimed our lines. On the night, just as Frank-N-Furter was to sing his mimed lines, the power went out, plunging us all into darkness much to the displeasure of the crowd of zoo staff and their families. All was restored within minutes and the show went on with a massive response at the end. A great night was had by all, and the following year due to our show's popularity, *Grease* was performed at the same venue. As the evening was captured on film it will remain as my one and only performance on record.

We would assist the Catering Department with weddings, where most couples would have their special ceremony in the Japanese Garden. It was a peaceful area within the zoo, apart from the aspect of vehicles travelling past the garden in the adjacent off-limit area. Sometimes just as the lovely couple were getting to the "I do" part of the proceedings, a beeping truck would drive by drowning out those special two words. Some or most couples would pay for the added experience of experiencing a giraffe feed, where the bride's bouquet was made up of edible food items that giraffes love. So with the giraffe bouquet in hand, and one of us standing next to them, they would have the giraffe eating and slobbering all over them, with us making sure that we were not photographed as part of the bridal party. One such couple after taking their vows, turned up wearing thongs, we were all impressed and charmed to say the least. This event was always popular and would provide us with some opportunity for easy and sometimes entertaining overtime.

CHAPTER 24

Feral Intruders

The Zoological and Acclimatisation Society of Victoria amalgamated with the Zoological Society in 1861. The Society was responsible for the introduction of starlings, sparrows, and the European Carp, as well as Samba Deer, rabbits, foxes, partridges and peafowl, and quail and guineafowl into Australia. Vast areas were soon overrun by rabbits and all these introduced species thrived. The Victorian Governor was quoted as saying "If the real objective of the Acclimatisation Society were carried out, not a single creature would remain in our charge for they would all be dispersed about the country". A truer word was never spoken. The zoo has for many years had to deal with feral species, mainly foxes and birds.

Many years ago a senior staff member stayed overnight within the zoo, positioning himself near a tea tree fence, an area where a fox had frequently been seen. Armed with a shot gun the keeper tolerated the cold, and at 4am the local milkman who then made deliveries to the zoo walked right past him without him seeing him at all. The feral intruder was not sighted that night.

On another occasion the same senior staff member was contacted one night by the Assistant Director to investigate an alarm that had been activated in the Zoo's Kiosk. On arriving another senior staff member was on the scene, and as the lights had been left on, they assumed that this was the reason for the alarm being activated. The police had been called and one soon turned up with pistol in hand. As they could hear someone approaching the call went out "Are you the Police?" The officer got such a fright his hat fell off his head and he crouched on the ground ready to discharge his firearm. "I could have shot you!" came his reply, when he realised that they were both members of staff, upon which one quickly replied, "I saw you first". Later two kids were apprehended in the adjoining parklands as they were the real reason for the activation of the alarm.

It was always a problem at the zoo when it came to feeding animals in open enclosures, with introduced Indian Mynahs overwhelming food bowls, or rummaging through rubbish bins. At one time I expressed concern regarding the number of Indian Mynahs and seagulls raiding the food in the Meerkats exhibit and would spend a considerable amount of time shooing them off to give the Meerkats a chance to feed.

Large colonies of Grey-headed Flying Foxes from a colony in nearby Fairfield would raid fruits on trees within the zoo and surrounding areas some of them found as far away as Reservoir. The zoo also had to contend with European foxes that would get into the zoo and cause havoc. Even native possums would raid rubbish bins overnight, scaring the hell out of cleaners in the morning. The only respite from possums would be the odd Powerful Owl seen in the trees with the remains of a possum in its talons. Some Twilight evenings the floors of some cages would be moving with masses or mice or rats. The zoo has a Rodent Controller employed full time. Feral animals will always be around, and the rats and mice will never be eradicated but adequately controlled.

CHAPTER 25

Animal Antics and Odours

Yes, they had a way of either setting you up or just plain embarrassing you, just by them or you being in the wrong place at the right time. So here are a few Animal Antics:

Tapirs are a herbivorous mammal from South America. They have a proboscis or short trunk, and a huge or should I say enormous prehensile penis that they use to keep hold of a female prior to copulation. I have lost count of the numerous times I would be in with our Tapir only for him to give the public a presentation of his gigantic organ, only to hear children asking their parents or teacher what it was. And if the question was directed towards me, well my capacity to not hear that well or not at all would come into play. One woman asked a keeper as to why tapirs have five legs? I believe she was taken aside by one of her friends to explain that it was not a fifth leg but used for a different purpose other than walking.

And another penis antic was carried out by our long-time resident Max the Mandrill, Mandrills are primates with a blue and red face, and are the largest of the Baboon family. Max would wait for the crowd to gather in front of the enclosure on busy days and weekends and when he had a considerable audience, would walk up to the log positioned at the front and rub his penis on it, much to the disgust of the crowd. You only had to hear the crowd's reaction from a distance to know what he was up to.

Our resident Leopard Cat, Lois, one of the smallest species of small cats, would calmly sit very close to you watching you hosing and going about your business, only to turn into a raging ball of fury if you got too close or attempted to catch her up.

One of the otters in a display near the main entrance would place her paw under the front viewing glass and scream pretending to be caught up, only to have a go at anyone who came up to attempt to free her.

A female otter decided while I was in the display feeding them, that the area just above my gumboot was more appealing, and she delivered a nasty bite filling my gumboot with blood.

A giant tortoise that took pleasure in walking up behind an unsuspecting keeper raising himself as high as he could and then lunging forward sending the keeper skyward.

While cleaning a Baboon cage the young Baboons would be allowed to stay out of the lock up area. As a keeper was cleaning, one of the young Baboons jumped on the inside of the cage gate and with it hanging off the gate it opened giving the young Baboon the opportunity to flee. As the keeper was hosing at the time he asked a visitor who was witnessing the event if he would just step over the barrier and close the gate for him, which the visitor did with the Baboon still attached, and restored to captivity. On another occasion a keeper was asked by a member of the public as he was cleaning a Baboon cage, "Is it OK to go in with these animals?" and upon looking up the keeper noticed that all the Baboons were sitting in the corner looking at him, dismayed at him being in with them.

One of the island enclosures in the zoo housed a rather aggressive gibbon named Yansi that hated keepers. The only way to service the island was to row across to close proximity to the island and with the use of a long pole depositing his food on a tray for him keeping a safe distance at the same time. The gibbon feeling rather adventurous this day walked along the feeding pole and deposited himself on the boat with the keepers. Through some quick thinking by one keeper the gibbon was safely returned to his island without any injury however this was not the case for the keeper who sustained a nasty bite to his foot. Who said that we are smarter than them?

One of the most significant things that remind you that you are working with exotic species is their odours, some that stay with you for the whole day. It's not just the odours but also from their behaviours and antics. Take the Mandrill for example, one of the largest of the Baboon family with the males having distinctive blue and red faces as well and posteriors. Mandrills smear their faeces on logs and other surfaces including the walls, floors and benches of their dens. Leaving us to clean up their creative artwork.

Lions have a distinctive odour as a way of announcing themselves. Lions define their territory by scent marking as most animals do. They spray a combination of urine and scent from glands at the base of their tails. They can spray urine backwards up to 6 meters and back up to bushes or in some cases spraying unaware members of the public, something for them to take away as a souvenir of their zoo visit. Binturongs have an odour almost like popcorn, this odour originates from chemicals in their urine which again is used to mark their territory and find a mate. They squat while they urinate so they can cover their feet and tails in it.

Giraffes have a very strong odour which is part of their defence system against parasites. Males are often called 'stink bulls' due to two highly odoriferous compounds.

Male Gorillas have a musky smell as they have large scent glands that they lubricate the palm of their hands and soles of their feet with. The one time you would notice how much of an odour you were wearing was when you would be driving home in the confines of your car.

I could go on in reference to many other odours that animals exude, maybe your next visit to the zoo will give you something to look or smell out for. Who knows you may even get the comment of, "Excuse me. but are you wearing Lion?"

CHAPTER 26

Bites and Other Bruises

As a keeper you would inevitably be in the line up for a bite or injury of some kind, and it was always human error even though at times it was accidental.

One bite came out of the blue from a Ring-tailed Lemur. I was fortunate and wise enough to move my arm away rather quickly as their razor-sharp teeth can do considerable damage.

While servicing a display I fell awkwardly against a padlock that was at ground level, splitting open my carpal tunnel, the area where the hand meets the wrist. The wound was very deep, and I made my way up to the vet department, which was not far away, to see the first aid person. I was in great pain and was holding the injured hand against my chest. They initially thought that I was bringing up a small, injured animal, but upon looking at my injury the first aid officer who was supposed to assure me that everything was OK yelled out in shock at the depth of the wound.

I was away from work for the best part of three weeks and the scar still reminds me of that day.

While servicing the pygmy hippo enclosure, I accidentally came into contact with the electric fence with my forehead, while bending over close to an embankment, resulting in not only a serious jolt but a serious headache. Another head injury resulted from hitting my head on the top of the giant tortoise's steel night den door resulting in several sutures to close the wound.

To clean the viewing windows in the hippo pool we would wear waders, as the water was chest deep. Not seeing some rocks on the bottom of the pool I fell forward, resulting in waders full of water and having my pride hurt as the public looked on at my humorous efforts to get out of the pool, looking like Sponge Bob Square Pants.

There were other minor injuries and incidents that occurred over the many years such as being stung by numerous European Wasps that would hide underneath the meat while we fed the big cats. That one I am sure other keepers could relate to. Other keepers over time, as with me, had injuries inflicted upon them. One had as I had previously mentioned had his leg torn open by a Lace Monitor while feeding them, another had a serious leg injury inflicted by a male Tapir. One of my work colleagues while restraining a Golden Cat had his hand badly mauled and had to undergo a series of operations to repair serious nerve damage. There has never been any fatal incidents at the zoo due to its excellent safety programme and occupational health and safety practices.

CHAPTER 27

Capture and Restraint and a Visit to the Vets

A situation would often arise where an animal would have to be sent to the veterinary department for treatment, or to be checked by the vets prior to shipment to another zoo. Some members of staff would be invited to be involved, or to witness such a procedure under supervision. It would also give the opportunity to video the event for training purposes. It was of utmost importance that this event was planned in advance with all staff members involved knowing their role and what was expected of them. Changes to work routines such as this could be difficult, or be a pathway to errors so it was always important to have a plan A and plan B. In one case a Polar Bear woke up on the vet table, as did a Gorilla. Swift action was taken on both occasions, resulting in safe and effective outcomes for staff and animals. That's why it was so important to have it all down to several game plans, with meetings held with everyone who was to be involved. I can recall having an adult otter in my hands, after being vet checked. As it had not fully recovered from the anaesthetic I was keen to get it into its carrier box. Otters are very flexible and can almost turn inside out to quickly deliver a nasty painful bite. As I had been bitten once before, I was eager to get this male off my hands. Just as it was becoming aware of its surroundings the keeper who was holding the box moved away from me suggesting that maybe we should put a blanket on the bottom of the box. My reaction was swift and loud, and my assistant immediately came back to within my reach with the otter being deposited into the box. Otters have thick insulated fur, they don't need blankets, but I would have needed some form of treatment if I had been savaged by the otter.

Many years earlier a Giant Anteater almost escaped from its transport box, as they have incredibly long and sharp claws which they use in the wild to tear open termite mounds for their favourite food. Luckily its escape plans were interrupted, and it was safely secured. If it had escaped I could not imagine how dangerous it would be to do a capture and restraint on a Giant Anteater.

Observing the behaviour of our charges was always a necessity, done first thing in the morning, and any changes would be reported to the veterinary staff, who would come down to have a look. It might be a lack of appetite with a carnivore which is always a concern, or maybe the way in which an animal was moving. If the issue persisted, or medication that was prescribed was not making any significant difference, then that was an indication for a visit to the Vet Department. Safety procedures are always based on routine, however in this case, being a change in the routine called for a briefing, re date and time for the animal in question to be anaesthetised and transported to the vets. Each staff member was allocated specific tasks to perform on the day, such as the Firearm Person, and who would assist with the moving of the animal, all areas were covered. The animal would be given no food prior to the procedure, and the vets would administer the anaesthetic with a dart gun. Once the animal was down and showing no signs of movement, the Firearm Person would enter the area first. Once on a stretcher and with a cargo net over it, the patient would be placed into the back of the vet's van and transported to the vet's. There would be someone who would walk in front of the van making sure that there were no people or obstacles in the way.

Once on the table the vet staff would take blood and perform a complete health check, checking eyes mouth claws etc. As it was not all that often that there was a big cat procedure of this kind, all angles were taken into consideration with nothing overlooked. Once treated or the problem rectified, it was just a matter of the reverse order in getting the animal back to its enclosure. Once the reverse drug was administered the vets and staff would observe the animal until it regained consciousness and was either sitting up or moving around. It was always a tense time for everyone involved.

CHAPTER 28

Tiger Rag and Golden Nuggets

Tiger Rag was a publication produced by a band of witty keepers and other staff members, for zoo staff. It contained an editorial, 'News from the Top', and included Management News, Animal News, Zoo Briefs, Vet News, an Education Report, as well as numerous cartoons, along with some poems, welcomes and farewells to staff, and a mixture of other stories relevant at the time. I can remember they included a copy of my 'late to work card' which read "Late due to Snake Bite". I wish the publication had lasted longer than it did. I still have a copy called 'The Bear Edition,' giving mention to the new bear and Coati enclosures, as well as comments and cartoons on the resident Food Store cat called Moog. It was a constant source of amusement to us all, and we would wait eagerly for the next edition.

Several members of staff were responsible for the Golden Nuggets, which was an evening of humorous skits on film, and awards presented in relation to what animals had been bred over the course of the year, and what memorable situations had occurred. The team could be seen at various locations in the zoo grounds filming during lunch breaks and even on their days off, with staff members being on guard for anyone looking on, as it was filmed in secrecy, only to be revealed on the night. One such skit was filmed in the newly opened bear enclosure, with the zoo gates closed and the visitors gone for the day, and the bears safely locked away in the off-limit areas. Several members of the keeping staff were filmed in the enclosure fully naked with fruit, vegetables and other bear food items scattered around them, and as they acted aggressively towards one another followed by the camera panning, passed a sign which indicated that it was 'A Bare Exhibit'. Other skits were filmed including one with me sticking my head into an empty snake enclosure, only to have many rubber snakes coming out at me, with the end scene showing me walking along with the rubber snakes attached to my face. A tribute if you could call it that to my rattlesnake bite incident. Other skits would show keepers riding their bikes into one of the lakes while watching women walk by, The Head Curator filmed while on his boat in the zoo grounds dressed in his yellow wet weather gear and keepers throwing buckets of water over him off camera as if he was in a storm at sea, only for him at the end of the water deluge to take off his wet weather gear to reveal him wearing a purple suit, and then heading off for another day in the zoo. Another involved filming three curators chasing an escaped butterfly down the main drive with huge hoop nets with the Three Stooges theme song playing in the background.

There was the Sneade Award which would be awarded every year at the event for the most highlighted stuff up perpetrated by a staff member. The Sneade Award was a keeper's boot standing on a toy stuffed penguin mounted on a log. There was also the Golden Nugget award for the department which had achieved the most notable breeding success, and other categories.

No-one was immune to the skits so cleverly filmed, not even the Director or other senior staff members who all took it in their stride and were always willing to make more funds available every year and to do whatever was asked of them on film for the event. Over the years as The Golden Nugget nights became so popular management made more funding available for the following year. Every year the event grew to such a level that it was a challenge for the staff involved to outdo the previous year. I became involved in some of the filming, but great credit should go to the major players for an event that was always entertaining. The Golden Nugget days are long gone and I still, as many would have, a smile on my face in retelling and recalling such a great event.

CHAPTER 29

Conferences, Moaning Frogs, and T-Shirts

The Australasian Society of Zookeepers had a conference every year at various zoos throughout Australasia. I took on the task at first as the Small Zoos Membership Officer where it was my task to get as many small zoos to join the Society as possible.

I later became President of the Society, a challenge I greatly enjoyed, and with the committee organised many conferences, in New Zealand, Sydney and Perth.

At one of the conferences at Taronga Zoo we ended up at one of the local pubs for a get together over a few drinks. Coming back to Taronga late one night after a serious drinking session with one of my Melbourne Zoo colleagues, we soon discovered that we could not get back into the caravan area that had been set up to provide cheap accommodation for the participants. So as not to wait for the security guard to come by we eventually decided to scale a nearby fence, which we managed to do quite successfully, considering our alcohol-fuelled condition. The following morning as we made our way to the conference area, we passed the point of our early morning entry, only to discover that we had not only been successful in scaling the fence, but we had made our way unscathed through the Alligator Enclosure. At an Auckland conference one of our staff members fell asleep on a couch in a reception area after a heavy session, he was not staying at our hotel and if it wasn't for the ASZK name badge he had around his neck he would have found himself out on the street.

It was the year for Perth Zoo to host the conference and keepers would apply as they did for any interstate or overseas conferences for financing from the zoo to cover airfares, accommodation etc. Keepers from the host State would usually provide accommodation, sometimes putting up several keepers within their homes. Most times we would prefer to just head home after a day's session to have a few drinks at our hosts abode, that way we didn't have to worry about getting home, like the time we jumped into a taxi and we could not remember the name of the hotel that we were staying at. As luck would have it the taxi driver knew most of the hotels in the immediate area and came up with the name of the one we were staying at. One evening we had to put one of our hosts to bed after a heavy night, we kept propping him up on the edge of the bed, only for him to repeatedly fall on the floor. After many attempts we finally got him between the blankets. That night as I reached down to pull up some disarranged blankets, I somehow managed in my state of semi-consciousness to grab the family cat, which I might add was not all that impressed. One evening we went frog hunting with torches in hand, scouring the nearby streets. The amphibian we were searching for was the ground dwelling insectivorous Moaning Frog. The male in pursuit of a female will call out in what could be described as a mournful moaning sound. With the Head Keeper from Melbourne Zoo we both ventured out into the backyard to hear the mournful moaning, only for her to inform me that she could not hear them due to the distant motorbike sounds, and wanted to wait until the sound abated, upon which I had to inform her the sound was in actual fact the sound of the frogs.

At a conference at Auckland Zoo, while I was introducing one of our guests from The World Wildlife Fund prior to his presentation, I was rather concerned about his appearance prior to his presentation as he was sweating and looked most uncomfortable. During his delightful presentation he proceeded to peel off one Wildlife T shirt after another and throw it into the crowd. I calculated that he must have been wearing about ten T shirts. No wonder he was looking as though he might be about to faint.

We would often find ourselves in numerous bars and night clubs with colleagues. Most bars and night clubs were well operated with no fighting tolerated and the food and service being first class, as well as the music. I would be amazed at some of the clubs when it was pointed out to us that the gorgeous barmaid behind the bar was a drag queen. At one Sydney conference after being in a bar with several keepers the night before I was to chair the morning session. The first presenter was to present a paper on the hand raising of kangaroos. He had disappeared during the evening and with minutes to spare he turned up looking rather worse for wear but nonetheless got up on the podium to give an excellent presentation.

On arriving at the airport to fly out to a conference in Auckland the crew from Healesville had rented a bus and arrived before we did with the plan for all of us to meet at the international bar. Upon arrival it became obvious after a while that one of the Healesville delegates was missing only to be found asleep under one of the tables. At the same conference our last day was the first day of presentations of the association of zoo directors as things were getting rather tight for us to see the sites of Auckland we left after the first session with some delegates getting a firsthand experience at bungee jumping.

At one of the Melbourne conferences we managed to acquire sponsorship from Cascade Breweries, whose emblem was the Thylacine, or Tasmanian Tiger, the same emblem as The Society. This resulted in free beer being provided for the conference, and good exposure for Cascade whose emblem we published in colour on the back of our journal, aptly called *Thylacinus*, which is part of the Latin name for the Tasmanian Tiger.

As well as receiving funds from the Zoos management, we would hold various events to help raise funds to assist keepers to attend conferences.

In order to raise these funds we would contact antique shops and ask them to donate animal related objects that we would pick up and offer for sale at the auction nights, where keepers and their families could bid for items that took their fancy. These and other events would raise anywhere between $2500 to $3000 for the Society.

The Society was a great vehicle for keepers to present papers and allow them to touch base with keepers throughout Australasia, and be aware of developments in the Australasian region. Many articles relating to captive breeding or husbandry issues were published within the society magazine. It also gave us the opportunity to compare notes and put names to faces and also to socialise. At a Perth conference at the end of the first day of papers and presentations, a marquee was set up with large bins full of ice and alcohol, much to the delight of us all. We also would be able to tour the zoo's that held the conferences and get some great ideas and experiences from them.

We also had for some years ANGFA – Australian New Guinea Fishes Association – conferences held at the zoo where we would have international guests, present papers and presentations. Later we would conduct tours throughout the zoo and behind the scenes experiences for the delegates.

A huge amount of time and effort went into all the zoo conferences, and it was always a great opportunity to re connect with other keepers from our sister zoos and compare notes and experiences at the same time parting with valuable knowledge.

CHAPTER 30

Koi, Burgers and Giant Gouramis

It was decided after looking at the state of the large pond in the Japanese Garden, that it was time for a clean out, as over the years visitors had thrown litter into the water and several semi-aquatic plants needed trimming and removing. The garden was built to recognise the sister state relationship with Aichi prefecture in Japan. In Japan an Australian garden was created in Nagoya Aichi. The garden was within a nice alcove of the zoo, with a Japanese gardener assisting the Horticultural Staff with its construction. It had natural rocks located at various levels along the stream to the main pool, which originated from a waterfall.

I took on the task of catching up the resident Koi fish and transferring them to some unused off-limit holding pools which had previously been set up to accommodate them, while the much-needed renovations were completed. Now Koi are significantly larger than the normal standard Goldfish, although they do look similar in appearance. Koi grow to around 90 cm and can weigh as much as 16 kg, quite a considerable size. They have a huge range of stunning colours and patterns and are much prized in Japan with some specimens fetching thousands of dollars.

After setting up the off-limit pools, we had to wait for several weeks prior to the move to allow the water to go through a cycle process. After testing safe to accommodate the Koi, it was time for the move. Large fibreglass containers were loaded onto a tray truck and during the early hours of the morning we commenced the transfer. We had lowered the level of the lake so we could venture into it with waders and make it easier to catch the Koi in large nets. As I was first to enter the water, I was soon rewarded by the discovery of a $50 note caught on a branch near the water's edge. A case of first in first served. The process at times was slow and stressful, and we took several hours to complete the task. Once all the Koi were swimming around comfortably in their temporary pools, we completely drained the remaining water from the lake and the horticultural team set to work. I with the vets checked the condition of the fish during their transportation and after they were returned.

This however reminds me of the day when we transported some carp from Werribee Zoo to the Hippo Pools, with the aim of making the public aware of how environmentally damaging carp can be, destroying the natural rivers and waterbodies of the world by stirring up the bottom of lakes etc making it considerably more difficult for endemic fish species to survive. There was only one problem, for some mysterious reason someone in charge decided to empty the pool that the carp were to be placed in, thinking maybe that it needed a good clean. Thus we found ourselves having no alternative but to place the carp in untreated water. Being a very tough and robust fish they all survived the ordeal. much to everyone's relief.

It was an unexpected call I received at the zoo one day from a hamburger outlet in Eltham where I lived. They sometime ago had two large aquariums installed in the premises, and they were having difficulty with the equipment and some of the fish. As it involved rather an urgent situation, I visited the outlet on the way home and found it to be indeed rather serious. South American Oscar Fish in the tank, which are considered to be hardy, were showing signs of stress due to the condition of the water and the lack of food, as were the other occupants. After some discussion with the Manager he offered me the position of Aquarium Maintenance man and a substantial wage to go with it. Now with working at the zoo and with my aquariums at home as well as other family matters to attend to, I was not in a position to take on this extra responsibility. I was at the time a member of the Australian and New Guinea Fish Association and thought that it was good avenue for them to be involved. I presented the idea to the Committee, and it was agreed that the Association would not only maintain the aquariums but completely re-aquascape and restock them with species of native plants and fish, thus not only promoting native fish and the Association but having money paid to the society for its services, which would assist with the production of its magazine. The Australian New Guinea Fishes Association was formed in 1982 by a group of hobbyists whose interests were in the conservation, keeping, breeding and studying of native fish. Plants and fish were sourced from members of The Association not only throughout Victoria but other states as well. Soon we had dates and times set for the revival of the aquariums. Some eight people made themselves available for the work and it had to be done overnight when the store was closed, with the only staff member present being the overnight cleaner. It all ran to plan with everyone putting in and come dawn it was all completed with new substrate plants and rocks. As we had completely cleaned the aquariums and filters we could not introduce the fish until the water had gone through the chemical cycle. Several weeks later after the water was tested and proved safe we re-introduced the fish. All of this created much interest from staff and customers. We even made a presentation of it at our next conference. We had developed a roster for members to service the aquariums and receive free meals for their families in return. Many years later the aquariums were eventually shut down to make way for store renovations, but it all proved to be a great worthwhile project for all parties concerned.

I later became president of The Association and organised with the committee for the society to become incorporated. I also enjoyed some great conferences throughout Australia. I will always remain grateful to The Association who promote our beautiful native fish.

On another occasion the zoo received a call from a local aquarium that was closing its doors due to the owner retiring. He had within a large aquarium a 14-year-old Giant Gourami. For those of you not familiar with Giant Gouramis, they are endemic to freshwater habitats in Southeast Asia and can grow up to 61 cm in length and weigh up to 9 kg. As they were and still are a species that can no longer be imported into the country, we were interested in taking up the generous offer. The gourami had been imported prior to restrictions being put in place. As the zoo at the time was seriously looking at the representation of fish species it was decided to acquire the gourami. The overall plan was to transport the gourami to the zoo in a specially designed transport tank on a trailer. We had the assistance of one of the aquarists from Snobs Creek Fish Hatchery to oversee the move with me and other zoo staff. Snobs Creek Fish Hatchery was located in Eildon and was designed to breed a large number of fish in an enclosed artificial environment, also being involved in the development of fish eggs and proper water control such as oxygen levels, temperature, and disease control. The whole operation was to be filmed for a popular television show which would promote both the zoo and Snobs Creek.

Prior to the move an anaesthetic, tricaine methane sulfonate, was added to the aquarium to partially sedate the gourami so we could move her into the mobile tank. The zoo vets were present to check on her condition during the process. Her tank was then emptied, and with the stand was loaded onto a zoo trailer. Once back at the zoo the tank and stand were installed and filled with the same water we had carried back with us. The same procedure was carried out for the gourami to be placed back in her aquarium, in an off-limit area. The whole operation proceeded without incident. The plan to have a Gourami Aquarium constructed in the future, however, did not eventuate. Several managers rejected the proposal to have a single large aquarium constructed next to the otter enclosure with money that a wealthy businessman was willing to donate to the zoo to finance the whole project. I often think of how much better it could have been. After this episode I felt that to attempt to promote fish in the zoo's collection was a lost cause, and I was grateful that I had had a good go at it. However in spite of all this I did manage to get a community aquarium in the reception area of the zoo provided from a local retail aquarium, a small consolation for what could have been.

CHAPTER 31

Check Your Local Zoo Out

If it's been a while since you visited your local zoo, then I hope this book has and will inspire you to do so, and that you feel a connection with it through these stories told through the eyes of a keeper, maybe having a better understanding from the other side of the fence.

I wish there were no zoos and that we didn't have to accommodate species in captivity, but without them many of our known species would no longer be in existence. Many of them are vulnerable or threatened mainly by habitat destruction. Zoos are always challenging themselves, and us as well, to have a better understanding of the natural world. So a visit to the zoo can help to provide funding and support, maybe to join the zoo as a member and become involved with certain activities or workshops. It's always a pleasant day out to take in the sights and sounds and to have some idea of what goes on behind the scenes at your local zoo. And most importantly what programs they are involved with, such as:

'Fighting Extinction'

Zoos Victoria is fighting extinction via their conservation programs and delivering positive results for wildlife not only in Australia but overseas as well. The goal is to be the world's leading zoo-based conservation organisation, being actively involved in Mountain pygmy possums survival and protecting Papua New Guinea tree kangaroos, just to name a couple. Here are other programs that Zoos Victoria is heavily involved in.

'Not on Our Watch'

Zoos Victoria committed to ensuring that no local terrestrial vertebrate will become extinct. Some 20 species and subspecies that are on the verge of extinction have been identified in Australia, and without critical action by zoos they will become extinct. A fine example is the successful breeding of various species of frogs such as the Corroboree and Baw Baw Frogs, and other endangered species that could possibly be on the verge of extinction if not for the efforts by Zoos Victoria and its partners.

'They're Calling on You'

A major threat for Gorillas in the wild is the mining of coltan, a mineral product used in the production of mobile phones, so the recycling of mobile phones greatly reduces mining in Africa.

Mobile phone refurbishment assists in lessening the demand for coltan, and mining in Gorilla habitats. Money raised from donated mobile phones assists in supporting rangers in the Democratic Republic of Congo. The issue is that the majority of world's coltan reserves are found in Africa, and every phone donated helps the cause.

'Don't Palm Us Off'

Palm oil is found in numerous food products and comes from palm oil plantations in Asia. It is the biggest threat to Orangutans, as habitats are destroyed to make way for more plantations. Certified sustainable palm oil is the safe alternative, and this program encourages consumers to demand it, and only purchase products that contain it. Maybe send an email to the manufacturers of your favourite foods enquiring if it is sourced from sustainable produced palm oil.

'Beads for Wildlife'

In Kenya livestock and wildlife compete for precious water and food. Beads for wildlife provides alternative income for the women. By purchasing beads that the women produce supports their livelihoods, taking the pressure from the region's wildlife. Bead products are available for purchase online or in the zoo's shop.

'Seal the Loop'

Plastic pollution in our waterways and oceans is becoming more of a problem every year and is placing all freshwater and marine life at risk of entanglement, which inevitably results in the deaths of many penguins, seals and other inhabitants. The majority of plastics can be recycled and there are many groups that one can join or work as an individual to remove plastic pollution from our beautiful beaches and waterway environments.

'Wash for Wildlife'

Promoting phosphate-free detergents to reduce the impact on one of our most iconic animals, the platypus. Problems arise when there is excessive output of these products into our waterways. Phosphates are one of the main causes of pollution and you can make a huge difference by purchasing products that have a phosphate free label.

'Wipe for Wildlife'

Promoting the use of recycled toilet paper thus reducing the number of trees that are destroyed to produce such a product.

Many other programs will and have been put into place and the message in many ways being delivered via Keeper Presentations and via the media. To make us all aware that there are better alternatives giving a better outcome for us and all wildlife. So you can be involved in and with the zoo by supporting these important programs and spreading the word.

CHAPTER 32

So You Want to be a Keeper

It's not just a matter of stating that you love animals, which would always be the line I would get from someone who would express their interest in pursuing a zoo keeping career. Even today every now and then I'm approached by a friend who has a friend or relative who wants to get a job at the zoo, and asks how do they go about doing that? Well, it's easier said than done, but not a matter of mission impossible. It just takes time and determination.

Many years ago one particular individual walked into the zoo and managed to have a meeting with the Head Curator, and after almost an hour of constant talking he walked out of the curator's office with a keeping position. I wish it had been that easy for me all those years ago.

Many years ago there were no academic courses that you could pursue directly related to zoo keeping. Some successful applicants had previously worked in other zoos, wildlife parks or animal labs. Today one can get experience by volunteering at your local vets, animal welfare organisations, maybe at the local catteries or kennels.

Today to be considered for a zoo keeping position, applicants must first be accepted into a preferred keeper list or pool. This selection process involves a workplace assessment. Then once a zoo keeping role becomes available candidates from that preferred list are eligible to apply. Short-term contracts are offered to the preferred keeper listings as the roles become available and can range from a few weeks to a year. Zoo keeping is physically demanding, and you need to have a good level of fitness. It's a lot of walking, raking enclosures, shovelling and lots of repetitive work and your standards need to be high. Applicants are even tested on running abilities, push ups, core muscle, grip, and lower back strength, as well as a full health check.

The Zoo Keeping course is extensive and includes many modules covering subjects such as Occupational Health and Safety, Captive Husbandry, Health, Nutrition and feeding, Reproduction, Enclosure Design and Maintenance, Genetics and Behaviour, just to name a few of the total sixteen modules. Certain other requirements are required, one of which would be the ability to work well with others as part of a team. We would have applicants come into the zoo and be put through assessment sessions, working together to solve a puzzle, and we would observe their individual reactions and behaviours according to each task. Some other tasks were set up in off-limit areas, involving raking up elephant faeces, to assess how they would approach this task using the tools and wheelbarrow. Cutting up buckets of fruit and vegetables, how they handle this, are they adaptive or hesitant. This would usually run for one day with only a handful of applicants selected. From here they would be the core to fill future fixed-term positions, and as they would progress be given as I have previously mentioned the opportunity to apply for a full-time position. So it's a tough road to take to become a full-time keeper, but a rewarding one, nonetheless. It's also important to note that keepers work as a team and look out for one another and maintain high levels of safety. Excellent communication is essential and can mean the difference between life and death and I know that sounds rather extreme but it's a fact.

CHAPTER 33

My View on Zoos

There are two International zoos I have visited over the years that I was most impressed with, considering that I look at zoos through the eyes of a keeper and can be critical when it comes down to it.

The first is Jungle World at the Bronx Zoo in New York. This indoor rainforest contains rare and interesting species such as Malayan Tapirs, Indian Gharials, Tree Kangaroos, Javan and Silver Leaf Langurs, White-cheeked Gibbons, and a multitude of tortoises and fish including Giant Gouramis.

The other is the Tropics Gallery at Vancouver Aquarium, equally as impressive with sloths, Caimans, giant fish, freshwater stingrays, Squirrel Monkeys, and a myriad of other species. Warm rain falls from time to time and cloud shadows drift across the ceiling.

These are perfect examples of habitat immersion, where it is difficult to believe that these are inside large areas, and with the combination of subtle dioramas on the walls gives it a brilliant illusion of depth of field. Live plants of numerous species grow in all areas and artificial branches of trees look life like with twists and turns and vines and creepers. It's a stimulation of the senses, sight, smell and sound at times having you believe that there are no barriers.

Enrichment items are only used in the off-limit areas, there is no need for them elsewhere, as there is more than enough within the environments to stimulate and enrich the inhabitants. There is some interpretation but not much, as this would take away the effect of everything being in the wild and you in it with them. Visitors learn so much about the animals within just by experiencing such environments. They have to, without knowing, work to see maybe just a glimpse of a primate or reptile. Visitors spend more time looking and being in awe of what surrounds them. Maybe inspiring them to look at the plight of natural habitats and what can be done to protect them.

Visitors learn so much from this experience and they will often come back to the Rainforest to see if they can get a glimpse of an animal. Visitors have to work for what they see as they would in a wild environment. It is warm and sometimes hot in some of these areas and the animals react to these changes.

Enrichment is an important tool, but to see items in an enclosure without the appropriate signage would be looked upon as maybe something negative rather than positive. We have come a long way from the concrete, cages, bars and wire of the 1800s that would be looked upon today as prisons. The concrete enclosures then had a diorama painted on the back wall depicting a rainforest for a lion, not a pride of them but just one, with the whole complex giving the observer a feeling of safety and power over the lion. Something to laugh at or throw things at, belittling the very aspect of the animal. Some animals were looked upon as beasts, pacifists, or some other name. Some calling the lion's mouth 'the jaws of death,' a term a circus would use to attract patrons into the Big Top. Bears were viewed by looking down on them with only a pool or concrete cave to get away from the oppressive heat. They would stand on their hind legs begging for a treat, that they didn't get more often than not. It was the place to go or be seen on a Sunday, with adults dressed up in their finest clothes.

Zoos have come a long way since then, providing more naturalistic enclosures or open areas without the overhead wire or bars. But we know that every animal will be visible to the visitors to avoid any complaints. What the visitors want, and what we provide them with, can lead to expectations dashed on the shores of disappointment if there are fewer animals and some of them cannot be seen. This is not a reflection on zoos for that matter, but what is it that we have to be more aware of that we can offer the visitors? What messages do we want them to take away with them after their visit? Melbourne Zoo's Butterfly House is a great example of immersing the visitors in a tropical environment with no constraints on the butterflies or the visitors, and for them of having the thrill of a butterfly landing on them. There was or maybe is more with some Tropical birds added to the experience.

After visiting Jungle World and the tropical rainforest in Vancouver I was amazed at how it stimulated me, and spent hours within it constantly discovering new things as one would in the wild.

As I look back at the way in which we did things at Reptile and Fauna Reserve all those years ago, I sometimes shudder at the fact that I survived it all, without becoming a statistic. And went on to bigger and better things at Melbourne Zoo where I was instructed by the best and passed on what I had learnt and experienced to future generations of keepers.

My daughter works with the Cat Protection Society in Greensborough as Foster Manager and I am amazed at the high standards of the facility when I visit from time to time, and although she did not follow exactly in my footsteps she has the same qualities that I had: passion, commitment, and thc drive to make the life of the domestic cat a better one, and giving cats another chance at life.

Anthropomorphism

Anthropomorphism, as you may well ask, is defined as giving human characteristics or behaviour to an object or an animal. Let me give you an example: I once saw an image of several penguins at Christmastime being walked down a main drive of a European zoo wearing Santa suits. This image not only horrified me but disgusted me. Penguins don't celebrate Christmas or birthdays as we do so it's not appropriate to dress up any type of animal and believe that it's acceptable, when what we are really doing is degrading the animal. We may celebrate certain important events in our lives but what we celebrate just doesn't come into an animal's life.

So we can see the use of anthropomorphism with companies selling their wares using Meerkats or some other animal. The danger of this can be that we misinterpret it and want to see Meerkats at the zoo due to us seeing them in these ads, or to see them for what they really are. So maybe that's something to think about as to the way we see the animal world through realistic eyes, or ones that are clouded by anthropomorphism.

CHAPTER 34

My Final Farewell

My very last day at Melbourne Zoo was full of surprises. Rather than having to do any work, I was given the full day to revisit departments I had worked in over the years, spending time with keepers and animals alike. I walked around the zoo later on in the day, allowing memories of times gone by to come flooding back to me.

On the day of my official farewell the staff had spared no expense, and the amount of time and effort that was put into it was amazing. The event was held in the boardroom and a photo board had been set up, filled with images to remind me of my zoo journey.

The CEO, Director and numerous other staff members came along to say their goodbyes, it was for me a very emotional time. Days before the farewell event the hat had been passed around to buy me a farewell gift. I wanted that money to go towards something significant to me, and I asked and was given time to think about what I wanted. It had to be something to keep that would remind me of my 33 years' service at Melbourne Zoo.

I have always admired Pamela Conder, a widely recognised wildlife artist, and wanted, if possible to have one of her works. In contacting her she was more than happy to allow me to select one, with the money from my collection hat to go to tiger conservation. My wife and I visited her home to look at what she had available. On looking at one of her portfolios, I kept coming back to a tiger sketch, and it was no surprise to her when I selected it. Many years prior Pamela had an art exhibition at a gallery very close to where I lived, I visited the gallery numerous times and was amazed at one of the paintings of a tiger. The tiger painting in question was the mother of Frank, a tiger that I had looked after at the zoo, so it was special to me. I didn't at the time have the finances available to purchase it, and when it sold I was devastated. The link to this story is that the sketch I selected that day was a sketch of Frank's father. So for me it had come full circle and today the tiger sketch is framed and takes pride of place on the wall at home, allowing numerous visitors to our house to admire it, and give me the chance to tell the story behind it.

CHAPTER 35

Memories For Keeps

I have always considered myself so very fortunate to have had a wonderful career working with a huge variety of animals and people at Melbourne Zoo, and to have been trained by the best and to have had the opportunity to train and pass on my knowledge to others. I will carry those experiences with me forever. Zoos play a very important part in allowing visitors to discover, learn and appreciate the natural living world which we need to allow to thrive on the planet that we share.

Practices over the years have changed from those we learned and experienced. Experience is a great but at times a harsh teacher, and as I look back at the way things were done and the way in which they are done today there is a vast difference. Safety practices today are just as rigorous as they were then. Staff are constantly reminded of them and carry out the safe routines to the letter. What we did all those years ago and the way everything is done today is in some ways the same. Melbourne Zoo has an excellent safety record based on excellent proven practices.

Life on the Other Side of the Wall

I don't use the words 'retired' or 'retiree', as I don't consider myself being in that category. I've pursued many interests since leaving Melbourne Zoo, such as gardening and a passion for creating aquatic and semi-aquatic environments in ponds and aquariums. I worked for just over a year at Totally Reptiles, an outlet in Greensborough where I got the opportunity to use my experience and skills working with an amazing group of people whose passion and knowledge always flowed from them. Totally Reptiles began as a single shop in Rosanna operated by the Prideaux family. Some years later it moved to larger premises in Greensborough. I had the opportunity in making and installing some changes to their Fish Room and other areas, once again working with Australian reptiles. I also discovered that the shop obtains reptiles from a breeder in Queensland with whom I worked with in the Reptile House at Melbourne Zoo all those years ago.

I'm also passionate about bromeliads, succulents and ferns, and I enjoy hours spent in our large Eltham garden. Many years ago I completed an art course over a period of some four years and have been fortunate to have sold many of my paintings, some overseas. I was given the task to paint some large reptile paintings for Totally Reptiles shop front when they established another new store in Kangaroo Flat. The walls of my art studio are covered with images of my Zoo journey. Historic photos of the zoo share that space as well as other items that I can surround myself with. There are many occasions I have taken time out to look at them at length and allow them to take me back to a time that, from where I now stand, passed in a flash. But what a flash that was, times that I was able to indulge myself in a passion that became a profession. I remember not all that long ago that I stood outside the place where it all began for me, and it looked vastly different after some 39 years.

The place is overgrown now.

Only the ruins remain of enclosures that once housed pumas, lions ... and a tiger named Karliff.

TO THE ONE WHO WAS ALWAYS THERE

I have written all of these accounts without mentioning many names. And although I have refrained from mentioning anyone, those work colleagues who read this will no doubt know to whom I'm referring to. It is here that I make an exception and the name of a person which stands out from us all.

Bev Drake, who was not only Keeper in charge of Native Mammals, but became Operations Manager at Melbourne Zoo, and a guiding light to all keepers. She was always there for us through both the good, sad, and tough times.

She sometimes knew us better that we knew ourselves and always practiced what she preached. We learned so much from her, and she could give us that push that she knew we needed. There are so many times I can recall when she was there for not only me, but for anyone within Zoos Victoria. She would always be ready to listen to what we had to say, or yell or cry about, then she would impart her wisdom upon us making us better at what we did. She would tell us how to capture a kangaroo or wallaby and then go out and demonstrate it. She could joke and laugh with us and join in with practical jokes. Her knowledge is vast and astounding, and everyone within the industry respected and loved her, and I am so proud that she is still part of my life and the very dearest of friends.

ACKNOWLEDGEMENTS

I wish to firstly thank my wife Mary Ann for her encouragement and endless hours of correcting and editing without which I would never have achieved this publication.

To Pamela Conder, for her support, her assistance in editing the manuscript, her invaluable advice, and her time willingly spent in so many discussions over the journey thank you so much.

I would especially like to thank Olga Dementiev and the professional team at New Holland Publishers for their belief that I had a story to tell.

To Melbourne Zoo for their permission to reproduce images taken within the zoo.

To News Corp for permission to reproduce photos previously published in the *Herald Sun* newspaper, and to Jay Town for his invaluable advice and support.

Last but certainly not least my thanks go to Ernie Webber, Bev Drake, Karen Svalesen, Ron Prendergast and Ian Freeman for their assistance and advice in providing important and relevant information. All of them at some time worked with me and I learnt so much from them and, as with all my fellow zookeepers, will forever be indebted for my time spent with them at Melbourne Zoo.

REFERENCES

Montagnana-Wallace, Neil (2012): *150 years Melbourne Zoo*, Melbourne: Bounce Books

Wilkie, A.A.W. with Mrs A.R. Osborne (1917): *Almost Human, Reminisces from the Melbourne Zoo,* Melbourne: Whitcombe & Tombs Ltd